Explosion of the Steamboat
SALUDA

Missouri River Steamboat Route (1850's)

Explosion of the Steamboat

SALUDA

A Story of Disaster and Compassion
Involving Mormon Emigrants
and the Town of Lexington, Missouri,
in April 1852

William G. Hartley
and
Fred E. Woods

MILLENNIAL PRESS
SALT LAKE CITY, UTAH

Millennial Press, Inc.
11968 S. Dove Landing Dr.
Riverton, Utah 84065

ISBN: 1-930980-74-4

For additional copies, call 1-800-217-4881.

Cover drawing by Buck Martin, used by permission of the *Kansas City Star*

Dedicated
to
the people of Lexington
and
Ruth M. White

Contents

Preface

The *Lexington Express* ran an "Extra" that trumpeted loudly the tragic events of April 9, 1852, in which the steamboat *Saluda* exploded on the Missouri River, near the shores of Lexington, Missouri:

> Twenty-six mangled corpses collected together, and as many more with limbs broken, and torn off, and bodies badly scalded—wives and mothers frantic at the loss of husbands and children—husbands and bereaved orphans engaged in searching among the dead and dying for wives and parents—are scenes which we can neither behold nor describe; yet, such a scene was presented to the citizens of Lexington on Friday—Good Friday—a day forever memorable in the annals of Christianity as the day that witnessed the redemption of man from endless death, will long be remembered by the passengers on the ill-fated Saluda, as a day of sorrow and privation. . . . the number of killed and badly wounded is about one hundred.[1]

This explosion marked what some would consider the worst steamboat explosion in the history of the Big Muddy.[2]

To know of the *Saluda* tragedy is to be fascinated by it. That's what happened to us authors, independently. After reading accounts by survivors, we became "hooked" on the story. In 2001, we agreed to combine our efforts and write a definitive history of the *Saluda*. Yet soon after our decision, the city of Lexington decided to sponsor a *Saluda* sesquicentennial commemoration in 2002. What better time to produce a book than for such an anniversary? Could it be done, though, in ten months? What follows is the best history we could generate within such a tight time frame, given our university workloads.

Records documenting the *Saluda*'s disaster are pooled in two locations, distant from each other. The archives of Missouri, where the tragedy happened, contain valuable newspaper accounts, court records, artifacts, and some firsthand accounts. In Utah, where many of the survivors went, libraries contain several accounts that they or their families wrote. Our extensive searches in libraries, museums, and newspapers and among descendants of

---

1   "The Explosion of the Saluda," *Missouri [Daily] Republican,* April 17, 1852, 2; reprinted from the *Lexington Express* for the date of April 13, 1852.

2   Life-time river man Phil E. Chappell, *A History of the Missouri River: Discovery of the River by the Jesuit Explorers; Indian Tribes Along the River; Early Navigation and Craft Used; The Rise and Fall of Steamboating* (Kansas City, MO.: Bryant & Douglas Book and Stationery Co., 1911), 87.

Saluda victims have generated fat files of information useful for this history. Availability of records, not bias, causes our story to give perhaps undue attention to the Mormon company aboard the *Saluda*—members of The Church of Jesus Christ of Latter-day Saints. Thus far our searches, which continue, have turned up few accounts by the non-Mormon passengers.

Several captivating questions swirl like hanging smoke around the *Saluda's* story: Who were the passengers on board at the time? How many? Where were they headed? What condition was the *Saluda* in? What caused the explosion? Who was to blame? How did Lexington residents respond to the tragedy? What became of the survivors? How does the *Saluda* disaster fit in with the general history of steamboating on America's rivers, particularly the Missouri? We have answered those questions as best we can, based on what records we have found. (In the Appendix, for example, we provide a new list of passengers for whom we have found names, and we include an explanation of the various casualty estimates.)

Our study owes debts to previous researchers of the *Saluda* story, particularly Dan H. Spies, Ruth M. White, and Geri Berbert. We appreciate insights and materials provided by Lexington historian Roger Slusher, the Lexington Historical Museum, the Lexington Historical Society, and museum and file materials at the Battle of Lexington State Historic Site. Brant Neer, Chairman of the *Saluda* 150 Commemoration Committee, gave us research help and advice, as did Michelle Neer of Lexington Heritage Tours.

We appreciate the help we received from the staff and holdings at the following repositories: Special Collections, Murphy Library, at the University of Wisconsin-La Crosse; St. Louis Mercantile Library at the University of Missouri-St. Louis; St. Louis Public Library; Missouri Historical Society Library and Collections Center (St. Louis); the *Waterways Journal* office library and photographs in downtown St. Louis; State Historical Society of Missouri at Columbia; Western Historical Manuscript Collection in the Ellis Library at the University of Missouri-Columbia; Missouri State Archives (Jefferson City, Missouri); St. Joseph (Missouri) Museum; Council Bluffs Public Library; LDS Church Family History Library, and LDS Church Historical Department Library and Archives (Salt Lake City, Utah); L. Tom Perry Special Collections, Harold B. Lee Library, Brigham Young University (Provo, Utah); and the Ohio River Museum (Marietta, Ohio), which also houses collections of the Sons and Daughters of Pioneer River Men. Our visual sense has been indulged by the striking paintings of steamboat scenes by artists John Stobart and Gary R. Lucy.

Joyce Holt of the First Christian Church (Savannah, Missouri), owners of the *Saluda's* bell, generously shared with us file materials regarding the bell. We thank the *Kansas City Star* for permission to use the Buck Martin drawing on the cover. Artist Kiki Melver generated the map and steamboat schematic drawing for this book. We also thank I. Whitney Thompson for the research help she provided, and we are grateful for the editorial assistance of Don E.

Norton, Ted D. Stoddard, and JoAnna Woods. We are indebted to the Joseph Fielding Smith Institute and the Department of Church History and Doctrine at Brigham Young University, our employers, for research time and travel support. Finally, we thank the staff of Millennial Press for supporting us in this endeavor.

We hope readers will send us new information or any corrections the story needs. Please contact either of us c/o Brigham Young University, Provo, UT 84602.

Prologue

When a steamboat's scruffy leadsman measured water depths and yelled out, "By the mark, twain," the captain knew the river was twelve feet deep and safe for travel. Gifted American writer Samuel Clemens, who grew up around river boats, adopted that familiar river phrase as his pen name, Mark Twain. When the *Saluda* tragedy happened, he was seventeen and living in Hannibal, Missouri, 140 miles east-northeast as the crow flies. Four years later he would become a steamboat pilot. Twain's stories more than any writings or art work preserve a feel for that bygone era when steamboats were America's primary interstate transportation mode.

To our generation, the old paddle-wheelers may seem romantic and nostalgic. But, in their day they were big business, being the nation's major interstate transportation mode for freight and passengers. River travel was risky. River steamers were subjected to decay, battering currents, floating debris, wind, rain, ice, fire, shifting sandbars, incompetent pilots and mechanics, and boiler explosions. Still, many river men, such as Captain Francis T. Belt of the *Saluda*, were willing to take the risk to gain a fortune. In 1848, four years before the *Saluda* disaster, *DeBow's Review* reported a tally of 233 explosions on steamboats during the prior four decades. The average life span for a Mississippi steamboat was five years, but a Missouri steamboat averaged only three. For the *Saluda*, which had sunk once already and had to be rebuilt, 1852 was her sixth year.

CHAPTER ONE

Costly Decision at St. Louis

The towering chimneys that reared up ahead of the pilothouse were identical tubes of sheet iron supported by cross-bracing. Each served . . . boilers, whose furnaces enjoyed a forced draft created by venting spent steam into the base of the chimneys . . . though now, of course, the fires were being damped down and the relief valves on the boilers set to their lowest. If steam were not regularly bled off there was the danger that a badly packed joint might spring a leak, or even that a boiler might explode. The boats which ran this river were very fragile.[3]

Scotsman William Dunbar, who would lose his wife and both his children when the *Saluda* exploded, had three opportunities to avoid passage on the ill-fated steamboat. Sadly, three was not enough. His first came when he and his family literally missed the boat in St. Louis.

William and wife Helen Reid Dunbar and children Euphemia, six, and Franklin Lorenzo, one, were part of a company of some 333 British Mormons—members of The Church of Jesus Christ of Latter-day Saints—who had crossed the Atlantic from Liverpool to New Orleans in the sailing ship *Kennebec* and reached St. Louis aboard the dilapidated steamboat *Pride of the West*. In St. Louis, the company split, some stopping there temporarily while the majority intended to head upriver to Kanesville, (present-day Council Bluffs, Iowa) to join wagon trains heading west to Utah Territory.[4] Of this seven-thousand-mile-long emigration from Liverpool to Great Salt Lake City, the steamboat leg was supposed to be the easiest—less demanding certainly than two trying months at sea or two arduous months of covered wagon life on the trail.

The Dunbars found, as did all river travelers that week, St. Louis's wharf district lined with docked steamboats, many of them idle. Packet boats, those that made regular runs up and down the Missouri, were not taking passengers

---

3 John Brunner, *The Great Steamboat Race* (New York: Ballantine Books, 1983), 28–29.

4 Beginning in 1848, and especially after the gold rush began, Kanesville, a Mormon town, became a major outfitting point for wagon trains because of its proximity to overland trails and its Missouri River location. Thousands reached Kanesville by Missouri steamboats to begin their western treks.

until icy river conditions improved. Late winter weather had sent fleets of ice chunks down the Missouri River from above Kanesville, making the normally dangerous push upriver extremely risky, if not impossible. But for the trail-bound emigrants, extended delays in St. Louis could handicap them severely. Extra lodging and meal expenses would drain the meager funds budgeted for the rest of their journey, and lost time could cause them to completely miss the wagon companies going west that year. But William Dunbar, had he stopped for longer, could have turned some of his fine singing and acting talents into meals, lodging, or cash. His mastery of bagpipes was novelty enough to attract a small crowd. But most of the other families in his company would not have fared as well.

William's friend, fellow Scotsman David Ross, recently had come down river from Kanesville along with Elder Eli B. Kelsey to help with Mormon emigration matters. Elder Kelsey, a seasoned church worker just returning from missionary service in England, felt urgency to book a steamboat for the Mormon flock. Working the wharf, he talked to shipping agents and boat captains, but all turned him down. He discovered that first-class boats would not leave for several days—until the river cleared. Finally, Kelsey spoke with Francis T. Belt, captain and part owner of the *Saluda*. Captain Belt, tempted by the potential profits from such a large block of passengers—in addition to others anxious to hurry upriver—decided his steamboat would brave the treacherous, ice-laden waters. Word along the docks rumored the *Saluda* was one of the less-desirable boats plying the river. Despite that, Elder Kelsey secured her on inexpensive terms and recruited Mormon emigrants for the trip. William Dunbar was one: "Going to the [LDS Church][5] conference office in St. Louis, I met my old friend, Brother Duncan Campbell, who, like myself, was a native of Scotland, and after consulting with him for some time, we both concluded, though somewhat reluctantly, to engage our passage, together with our families, in the Saluda."[6]

After signing up, he and friends Duncan Campbell and David Ross went down to look over the boat, which was still waiting to complete its booking of passengers for the trip. Going aboard and walking around, they felt some foreboding. At least that's what Dunbar said in the years afterwards:

> On entering the hold a most horrible feeling came over us, and without knowing the cause of it, we had an impression that something awful was going to happen somehow or other. We looked at each other in silence, then turned away in opposite directions, and when our eyes again met, we saw tears coursing their way down each others cheeks. Hurrying away from the boat, I remarked to brother Campbell that if I had not already

---

[5]   The Mormon acronym "LDS" is used to refer to members of The Church of Jesus Christ of Latter-day Saints. They are also referred to as "Saints."

[6]   Andrew Jenson, "Fifty-sixth Company—*Kennebec*," *The Contributor* 13, no. 9 (July 1892): 411.

given in my name to go with that steamer, I would not do so now; but under the circumstances we almost felt it duty bound to go, so as not to disappoint the officers of the boat, nor the Elders who had chartered her.[7]

Captain Belt planned to start the *Saluda* upriver the next day, so Dunbar hurriedly bought supplies and gear for the trail trek west. The merchant promised to set the goods on board early the next morning. "This, however, he failed to do," Dunbar said. But even when the *Saluda* did not leave that day as planned, because of river ice, the promised items still did not arrive the next day by the time Captain Belt ordered the *Saluda*'s engineers to start heating the boilers. Desperate, Dunbar rushed to the merchant's place and waited until the goods were finally sent. Then he and Helen and their two small children hurried toward the docks to get aboard the *Saluda* before it left. Before reaching the doomed vessel, they heard an ominous clanging of the *Saluda*'s massive iron bell: "When we got within a few blocks of where the *Saluda* lay, we heard her bell ringing, as a signal for starting, and quickening our steps I reached the boat with one of our children in my arms, just as they were throwing off the gangway, and starting. Looking back I saw my wife carrying our other child, hurrying on as fast as she could, but still some distance away. Consequently, the boat started without us."[8]

Missing the boat seemed to them disastrous, but in hindsight it was a stroke of good luck. Little did they realize the true disaster that yet awaited them. This was the first of three chances Dunbar would have to avoid the *Saluda* tragedy. Twice more, providence tried and failed to keep the Dunbars off the *Saluda*. Said Dunbar in retrospect: "Although I did not understand it then, I am perfectly satisfied now that some friendly unseen power was at work in my behalf, trying to prevent me from going on board with my family on that ill-fated steamer."[9]

By contrast, Abraham O. Smoot, an elder acting as a church agent assisting the Mormon company, felt a similar premonition and heeded the warning. He later recalled:

> I had a very narrow escape on the occasion of the "Saluda" disaster. I had purchased the supplies for my company to make its overland journey with, except cattle, at St. Louis and had decided to go farther up the river to buy the stock, when Eli B. Kelsey came to me to consult me in regard to chartering the Saluda to convey an independent company of Saints up the river. I went with him to examine the boat, and on finding that it was an old hulk of a freight boat, fitted up with a single engine, I strongly advised him against having anything to do

---

7   Jenson, "Fifty-sixth Company," 411.

8   Jenson, "Fifty-sixth Company," 411.

9   Jenson, "Fifty-sixth Company," 411.

with it. He seemed to be influenced in making choice of it entirely by fact he could get it cheaper than a better one; but in my opinion it seemed folly, for in addition to the danger of accident, the length of time likely to be occupied in making the journey would more than counterbalance what might be saved in the charge of the transit. However, he decided to charter it, and then both he and the captain urged me strongly to take passage with them, offering to carry me free of cost if I would only go; but I could not feel satisfied to do so.[10]

[10] Jenson, "Fifty-sixth Company," 413–14. James Linforth, ed. *Route from Liverpool to Great Salt Lake Valley with Steel Engravings and Woodcuts from Sketches Made by Frederick Piercy* (Liverpool: Franklin D. Richards, 1855), 10, explained that the LDS voyages that embarked in January and February of 1852 carried Perpetual Emigrating Fund passengers (meaning Mormon converts who were using a revolving fund to help bring them to the Salt Lake Valley). Abraham O. Smoot had been selected to go ahead of these groups and arrange for items they would need while crossing the plains. Linforth further points out that "it was also necessary that men of experience should be selected to accompany the emigrants to New Orleans, pay their passage up the rivers, and deliver them into Elder Smoot's hands. This was entrusted to Elder John S. Higbee, who sailed with the *Kennebec.*"

CHAPTER TWO

Who Was on Board the *Saluda*?

Under the master, and pilot or pilots, three officers on a river boat exercised significant authority: the first mate, who oversaw the crew; the chief engineer; and the senior clerk, who attended to matters touching money. Because they included the taking-on of cargo and the letting of cabin and deck space, it was the latter's name that customarily appeared with the captain's in advertisements.[11]

Today, St. Louis's long shoreline on the Mississippi River, crowned by a magnificent stainless steel arch, shows visitors little evidence that this once was the steamboat capital of western America. Other river cities have obtained and preserved steamboats and moored them for tourists to board and inspect, but not St. Louis. A steamboat replica housing a McDonald's restaurant is the only hint that once upon a time this riverbank (since reshaped) saw hundreds of riverboats crowd the wharfs yearly, and a forest of steamboat chimneys blocked views of the river.

By early 1852, when the *Saluda* booked its ill-fated company for upriver ports, St. Louis bustled with river business. It was the primary terminus and transfer port for freight and passengers heading up or down the Mississippi River and merging from the Ohio and other major rivers. Wharfs and docks sagged under the weight of barrels, bales, boxes, cases, luggage, horse-drawn wagons and taxis, ticket offices, warehouses, and thousands of businessmen, emigrants, boat crews, soldiers, and visitors.

Within this kaleidoscope of wharf activities, the *Saluda* was just another steamboat, trying to earn money for its owners. Idle, it earned nothing. Therefore, when Mormon elders offered to book nearly a hundred passengers, Captain Belt rounded up his crew. The *Saluda* would leave, he announced, on March 29. Quickly, a mass of human beings, each with a name and personality and life story, began loading themselves and belongings into the aging craft, unaware that by so doing, they were heading for an infamous date with history.

---

[11] John Brunner, *The Great Steamboat Race,* 35.

River Commerce at St. Louis

St. Louis was founded in 1764. By the nineteenth century, as today's stainless steel arch boasts, it served as America's "Gateway to the West." In 1849, the city's businesses flourished when people heading for California gold passed through. From St. Louis, 58 "fine steamers" plied the Missouri River, 75 the upper Mississippi, 150 the Ohio, 28 the Illinois River, 28 the Tennessee River, and 100 the lower Mississippi. Boats could not be built fast enough to handle the flow of passengers and freight.[12]

In that same prosperous year of 1849, the city suffered two catastrophes. The "Great Fire of 1849" destroyed twenty-three steamboats at the levee and fifteen city blocks.[13] Thousands lost their jobs. Then, emigrants from Germany and Holland, where cholera was raging, bore the dreaded disease to New Orleans, whence it spread upriver. St. Louis was hit harder than any other city in America. The outbreak forced businesses to close from May to August, except grocery and grog shops. By July 30, 4,547 cholera victims had been buried in the city since the first of the year.[14]

After the fire and the epidemic, the levee area was enlarged and continued to swarm with boats, "as many as 170 ginger-bread trimmed boats often jostling each other at a time along its six mile wharf."[15] Some believed the most impressive part of St. Louis was its hotels.[16] These provided temporary lodgings for thousands of immigrants, mostly Germans or Irish.[17] Census takers in 1850 counted 77,860 residents, nearly half being Germans or Irish.[18] By 1850, St. Louis had resumed being the "River Queen," the greatest inland port in the nation.

One notable German immigrant living in St. Louis was Louis Espenschied, a wagon maker. Hundreds of his wagons, assembled and unassembled, were loaded onto steamboats or barges behind the steamers for delivery to wagon trains poised to pour west on the overland trails. Among his regular customers were Mormon agents who bought wagons for the church's annual wagon companies that outfitted upriver.[19]

Gathering to Zion

By 1852, Utah Territory had become the permanent home for believers in Mormonism, with Brigham Young serving as church president. The

---

[12] Walter B. Stevens, *St. Louis, The Fourth City, 1764–1909* (St. Louis: S. J. Clarke Publishing Co., 1909), 566.

[13] Charles Van Ravensway, "Years of Turmoil, Years of Growth: St. Louis in the 1850's," *The Bulletin: Missouri Historical Society* 23 (July 1967): 303.

[14] James Neal Primm, *Lion in the Valley, St. Louis, Missouri* (Boulder, Colorado: Pruett Publishing Co., 1981), 174.

[15] Van Ravensway, "Years of Turmoil," 304.

[16] Van Ravensway, "Years of Turmoil," 305.

[17] Van Ravensway, "Years of Turmoil," 309, notes that by the end of the 1850s, the Germans made up over a third of the population of the city.

[18] Primm, *Lion of the Valley,* 165–66.

[19] Lloyd Espenschied, "Louis Espenschied and His Family," *MHS Bulletin* 18 (January 1962): 86–103.

Church of Jesus Christ of Latter-day Saints formally began in 1830 in upstate New York, founded by Joseph Smith, esteemed by his followers as a modern-day prophet. Among revelations he received and published are several that direct believers to gather together in order to establish a religious society and escape the impending calamities of the world. In 1830, such counsel stated: "Ye are called to bring to pass the gathering of mine elect; for mine elect hear my voice and harden not their hearts. Wherefore the decree hath gone forth from the Father that they shall be gathered in unto one place upon the face of this land, to prepare their hearts and be prepared in all things against the day when tribulation and desolation are sent forth upon the wicked."[20]

However, the forming of religious communities brought persecution. As a result, the church moved from western New York to Kirtland, Ohio (near Cleveland) and then on to northwestern Missouri, to Nauvoo, Illinois, and finally to Utah. From its beginning, the church sent out missionaries to share what for Mormons was a restoration of the true gospel of Jesus Christ. Converts were encouraged to move wherever the church's headquarters were located.

Beginning in 1840, Mormon converts in England began to "gather to Zion" by emigrating from Liverpool, England, on sailing ships to New Orleans, and then upriver to Nauvoo, Illinois. By the mid-1840s, the church had developed an exceptional emigration system whereby agents chartered sailing ships for the Mormon emigrants. Other church agents welcomed them at each port or stopping point, and mature leaders were placed in charge of each emigrating company. This method ensured that emigrants received assistance in obtaining tickets, ship quarters, customs requirements, medical inspections, and money exchanges, and in moving themselves and their baggage to the next water or land vehicles booked for them. Many a vulnerable emigrant, especially those not speaking English, escaped unscrupulous business agents, con-men, and thieves at the depots. Starting in 1848, the Mormon migration route went by steamboats from St. Louis up the Missouri River to outfitting points in Iowa, upper Kansas, and Nebraska. The stream of Mormon emigrants continued to flow until the end of the nineteenth century, and by then nearly ninety thousand known Latter-day Saint immigrants had "gathered to Zion."[21]

Mormons and St. Louis

From the 1840s to the 1850s, St. Louis served for Mormons as a vital transfer point or place to stop and earn money before continuing on. Back in

---

[20] *The Doctrine and Covenants of The Church of Jesus Christ of Latter-day Saints* (Salt Lake City: The Church of Jesus Christ of Latter-day Saints, 1981), 29:7–8 (hereafter cited as D&C). The date of this conference was September 26, 1830; the date of the organization of the Restored Church was April 6, 1830. Although it was known as the Church of Christ at the time of its organization, the official name of the Church was given on April 26, 1838 as The Church of Jesus Christ of Latter-day Saints, by which it has been known ever since (see D&C 20:1; 115:4).

[21] Conway B. Sonne, *Saints on the Seas: A Maritime History of Mormon Migration 1830–1890* (Salt Lake City: University of Utah Press, 1983), 137.

1838, Missourians, supported by the governor's order that the Mormons must be exterminated from the state, drove them out of their communities in northwestern Missouri. The Mormons then established a large river city at Nauvoo, Illinois. Forced from there in 1846, they moved as a group to the shores of the Great Salt Lake. Yearly, the church sent proselytizing missionaries throughout the states and to Europe. Their gospel message included Christian basics, such as faith, repentance, baptism, and receiving the Holy Spirit, but in addition it called for converts to "gather to Zion," which meant to wherever the main body of The Church of Jesus Christ of Latter-day Saints was located in America. As a result, after 1847, thousands of Mormons headed for Utah each year, the majority passing through St. Louis.

Despite the Missouri expulsion of Mormons in 1838–39, St. Louis, being a big and diverse city, provided a safe haven for anyone living there or passing through.[22] In early 1851, the St. Louis *Missouri Republican* reported that about three thousand English Mormons were in the city, "nearly all of whom are masters of some trade, or have acquired experience in some profession." The article further noted:

> Though these people have no other class or permanent posses-
> sion or permanent interest in our city, yet their numerical
> strength here is greater than may be imagined. Our city is the
> greatest recruiting point for Mormon emigrants from England
> and the Eastern States, and the former especially, whose funds
> generally become exhausted by the time they reach it, generally
> stop here for several months, and not infrequently remain
> among us for a year or two pending the resumption of their
> journey to Salt Lake.[23]

In 1851, Mormon emigrant Jean Rio Griffiths stopped a few days in St. Louis and wrote a detailed description of its layout, markets, streets, and churches, including the Mormon congregations there.[24] St. Louis, she said, "is a large and fine city, extending 5 miles along the river side, and about half as far inland." After doing some shopping she noted: "The markets are extremely good, they open at four o'clock every morning except Sunday. All kinds of meat, poultry and fish are very cheap. The fish and meat is good, but not so large and fat as in the English markets. Vegetables and fruits are abundant and of great variety. Groceries, wines and spirits, are very cheap."

She said that the streets had raised sidewalks and stepping stones at intersections for pedestrians to use in crossing the street. Oxen were more commonly used than horses, except for private carriages. The city's places of worship were "magnificent buildings:"

22 Stanley B. Kimball, "The Saints and St. Louis, 1831–1857: An Oasis of Tolerance and Security," *BYU Studies* 13 (summer 1973): 489–519.

23 *Missouri Republican*, May 8, 1851.

24 "The Diary of Jean Rio Griffiths Baker," typescript, photocopy in authors' possession, entries for March 29 and April 4, 1851.

Let it belong to what denomination it may, [it] has a steeple and is called a church. The Catholics have three churches, each surmounted with a large gilded cross, the Presbyterians three, two of them splits from the first, the Baptists four, the Episcopalians and Independents several each, then there are the Methodists and Lutheran and Swedish churches, so that religions are as plentiful as can be wished. The poor despised sons of Africa too have a little church to pray and praise the Lord in, but it is only lately that their masters have allowed them the privilege.

Although the *Missouri Republican* that spring said the Mormons had no congregation in St. Louis, Mrs. Griffiths reported otherwise.[25] She found that her fellow Mormons "have six meeting rooms, they have also the use of the concert hall in Market Street on Sundays, which holds three thousand persons, and I could but feel amazed to see that spacious room filled to overflowing, and the staircase and lobby crowded with those who could not get inside. They have an orchestral band, and a good choir."

"Stop-over" Mormons, a St. Louis history noted, included many from England who "flocked in, setting up small shops, working in various crafts, or driving hackney coaches to replenish their finances for the final push westward."[26] Three years after the *Saluda* disaster, the Mormon population in St. Louis had grown even larger.[27] They held meetings in several places in the city and published a church newspaper, the *St. Louis Luminary*. In 1855, the *Luminary's* editor observed, "This city has been an asylum for our people from fifteen to twenty years. . . . There is probably no city in the world where the Latter-day Saints are more respected, and where they may sooner obtain an outfit for Utah."[28]

Emigrants aboard the Ship *Kennebec*

Four months before the *Saluda* blew up, the sailing ship *Kennebec* embarked from the Bramley Moore Dock in Liverpool, England, on January 10, 1852. As previously noted, on board this "unusually spacious and commodious vessel" was an organized company of 333 British Mormons.[29]

---

[25] *Missouri Republican,* May 8, 1851.

[26] Van Ravensway, "Years of Turmoil," 308.

[27] Kimball, "The Saints and St. Louis," 508–510, notes that in the middle 1850s, St. Louis had three thousand to four thousand Mormons and had formed a stake (diocese) there.

[28] *St. Louis Luminary,* February 3, 1855.

[29] "Sailing of the Kennebec," *The Latter-day Saints' Millennial Star* 14, no. 3 (February 1, 1852): 41–42. The passenger list indicates that of these 333 LDS passengers, 212 were adults, 107 were under the age of fourteen, and 14 were infants. Most of the converts were English, but they also included families from Scotland and Wales. For more information on this topic in general, see P. A. M. Taylor, *Expectations Westward; the Mormons and Emigration of their British Converts in the Nineteenth Century* (Ithaca, New York: Cornell University Press, 1966). Regarding Mormonism in Scotland in the nineteenth century, see Frederick S. Buchanan, "The Ebb and Flow of the Church in Scotland, 1840–1900," *BYU Studies* 27 (spring 1987): 27–52. For the story of the early Welsh converts, see Ronald D. Dennis, *The Call of Zion: The Story of the First Welsh Mormon Emigration* (Provo, Utah: Religious Studies Center, Brigham Young University, 1987).

Among them, sixty-nine were the first foreign converts financially helped to emigrate by the church's Perpetual Emigrating Fund, which provided loans and subsidies.[30] Because not enough Mormons were on board, eighty-five Irish emigrants became their fellow travelers.[31] Mormon elder John S. Higbee served as president of the Mormon group.

Their nine-week journey to New Orleans was pleasant but not without problems. One day a "terrific hurricane . . . swept the deck clean of cook houses, water barrels, and everything else that could be washed overboard."[32] Passenger James May, who would be on the *Saluda,* said it was "a long rough voyage" and "before the end we were out of food and water." John Spiers, an assistant to President Higbee, said that the captain declined an offer from the pilot at the Balize to take the *Kennebec* over the bar at the mouth of the Mississippi, so the tugboat left. For ten days, the *Kennebec* was stranded. May reported that the passengers had only rice and oatmeal to eat, without salt, and used brackish river water to cook it in.[33] On February 22, *Kennebec* passengers thanked Higbee for his leadership and asked him to continue to be their president for the New Orleans to St. Louis run, and, nearing New Orleans, they entrusted him "to make the best bargains for us he could," meaning, apparently, for transport up to St. Louis.[34]

Docking at New Orleans

Passengers enjoyed seeing tropical plants, plantations, and homes as their boat pushed north toward New Orleans. One traveler a year earlier noted: "The houses of the planters are built in the cottage style, but large with verandahs on every side, and beautiful gardens. At a little distance are the Negro huts, from 30 to 50 on each plantation. . . . Groves of orange trees are very numerous, the perfume from which is very delightful. . . . Thousands of peach and plum trees are here grown wild and are now in full blossom. . . . The only thing which deteriorates from its beauty is the sight of the hundreds of negroes at work in the sun."[35]

The *Kennebec* stopped at New Orleans on March 13, 1852.[36] In 1852, *Conclin's New River Guide* observed that New Orleans was "the princip[al] city in the south, and the third commercial mart of the States" which brings

---

[30] Upon arrival in the Salt Lake Valley, they were expected to pay back their loans as soon as they could. Established in 1849, the Perpetual Emigrating Fund, or PEF, aided about thirty thousand LDS emigrants during the nineteenth century. See Fred E. Woods, "Perpetual Emigrating Fund," *Encyclopedia of Latter-day Saint History* (Salt Lake City: Deseret Book, 2000).

[31] "Sailing of the Kennebec," 41–42.

[32] Jenson, "Fifty-sixth Company," 408.

[33] Reminiscences of James May, LDS Church Archives, 9–10; Reminiscences and Journal of John Spiers, LDS Church Archives, 227.

[34] The Journals of George Henry Abbot Harris, February 22 and March 20, 1852, vol. 1, 69, LDS Church Archives.

[35] Jean Rio Griffiths Baker Diary, March 20,1851.

[36] *1997–98 Church Almanac* (Salt Lake City: Deseret News, 1996), 161.

together "the inhabitants of all countries, colors, and languages."[37] Situated about a hundred miles from the mouth of the Mississippi River on the east bank of a river bend, it was known as the "Crescent City." Thousands of immigrants came to America through New Orleans.

From 1841 to 1855, 17,463 Mormon emigrants, in seventy-nine companies, landed at New Orleans. During that period, the church had an organized congregation there, "consisting for the most part of emigrants detained there by lack of means to continue the journey to St. Louis."[38] In 1854, LDS Church President Brigham Young ordered Latter-day Saint ship companies to start using Philadelphia, Boston, or New York for an arrival port instead of New Orleans, thereby keeping Mormon travelers away from yellow fever and cholera and other river diseases that thrived in the hot climate found in the lower Mississippi region.[39] Fortunately, the *Kennebec* passengers were not struck with cholera or yellow fever on the ocean or at New Orleans, although many later became cholera victims that summer, upriver from Lexington.

Travelers passing through New Orleans were amazed by its blend of French, Spanish, and American cultures, its foods, its architecture, and its busy waterfront. English immigrant Jean Rio Griffiths wrote in 1851:

> The roads themselves are not kept in order as they are in London, they are not paved. Just now the weather is hot and dry, so in crossing them you sink in dust up to the ankles. . . . The city stretches on one side of the river for about five miles as near as I could judge, the whole of which length is one continued wharf of levee, as the French have named it. The ships and steamers lie 4 or 5 deep the whole length, and as close as they can be stowed. . . . The levee is not level . . . but of gradual descent from the houses to the river, and completely covered with bales of cotton and other articles of merchandise, leaving sufficient room for the drays, which are used for the conveying of the cargoes from the ships to the warehouses.[40]

It was unusual for a Latter-day Saint company to arrive and not be met by a church emigration agent. Agents had been stationed there since the arrival in 1848 of Lucius Scovil. Thomas McKenzie followed Scovil in the fall of 1849. Apparently, McKenzie had to leave, and his replacement, John Brown, did not arrive until December 6, 1852.[41]

---

[37] *Conclin's New River Guide or a Gazeteer of All the Towns on the Western Waters* (Cincinnati: J. A. & U. P. James, 1852), 116–17, Mercantile Library, University of Missouri-St. Louis. The Guide (p.120) also notes that the population of New Orleans in 1850 was 119,285.

[38] Andrew Jenson, *Encyclopedic History of The Church of Jesus Christ of Latter-day Saints* (Salt Lake City: Deseret News, 1941), 576–77; David Buice, "When the Saints Came Marching In: The Mormon Experience in Antebellum New Orleans, 1840–1855," *Louisiana History* 23 (summer 1982): 221–37.

[39] *The Latter-day Saints' Millennial Star* 16 (October 28, 1854): 684.

[40] Jean Rio Griffiths Baker Diary, March 21, 1851.

[41] Buice, "When the Saints Came Marching In," 229–32. Also, see letters appearing in the *Millennial Star* 12, no. 1 (January 1, 1850): 14 and 12, no. 14 (July 15, 1850): 217, which indicate that McKenzie was actively involved as an emigration agent in 1850 but which are silent concerning his emigration efforts after that year.

From New Orleans to St. Louis

At New Orleans, where the church usually had an agent to meet emigrants and lead them to a steamboat he had booked for them, no agent was there to assist the *Kennebec* Mormons. President Higbee assumed that responsibility. When the *Kennebec* docked, Higbee met with a Mr. Cook at the lower part of the city who "assisted me in getting a steamboat to St. Louis and bought provisions for the company." The boat was the *Pride of the West,* a boat, as it turned out, in worse condition than the *Saluda.* "She came down & took us aboard," Higbee said.[42] "Arrived at New Orleans," wrote Henry Ballard, soon to be a *Saluda* victim: "We left the same day going up the Mississippi River upon an old frail craft of a boat called the "Pride of the West." It might have been entitled to that name in an early day, but not then. It was chained together to keep it from falling to pieces and they kept her near the edge of the river all the way to St. Louis."[43]

They made a safe journey upriver, about 1,250 miles, on the risky old boat, except for a young man named Snedden who fell or was thrown overboard and drowned. His body was never recovered.[44] The river varied from eight hundred to fifteen hundred yards in width. At first, being out on the decks was not pleasant except in cloudy weather, but the farther north they churned, the cooler the days became. Passenger Robert Bell wrote that "we left New Orleans the 14 of March and arrived at St. Louis the 26 of Mar. making a long passage of 12 days."[45]

The *Saluda* Decision

Again, it was unusual not to find a Mormon agent waiting at the St. Louis levee to assist church members wanting to head for Kanesville. Nathaniel Felt had been the St. Louis agent from 1847 to 1850, with John Taylor, Franklin D. Richards, and Jedediah Grant rendering assistance during Felt's final year. However, when people from the *Kennebec* arrived, there was no local emigration agent present.[46]

Instead, Eli B. Kelsey and David J. Ross had been sent from Kanesville to fill in. Ross had come to America in 1846 and lived and farmed in the Kanesville and St. Joseph, Missouri areas. Then in the spring of 1851, church leaders assigned him to be an LDS frontier outfitting agent and in 1852 sent him to assist Eli Kelsey with the supervision of emigration matters at St. Louis and to the West. Kelsey had served a proselytizing mission to Scotland and had

[42] Reminiscences and Diaries of John Sommers Higbee, March 13, 1852, LDS Church Archives.

[43] Reminiscences and Diary of Henry Ballard, March 14, 1852, LDS Church Archives.

[44] Jenson, "Fifty-sixth Company," 408-10.

[45] Robert Bell, Correspondence, LDS Church Archives, 2.

[46] Newly appointed emigration agent Horace S. Eldredge wrote in his journal that he left Salt Lake for St. Louis with John Brown, the newly assigned emigration agent in New Orleans, on September 15, 1852, and "landed at St. Louis," November 19, 1852. See Journal of Horace S. Eldredge, September 15 and November 19, 1852, LDS Church Archives.

recently returned to America. Ross and Kelsey traveled together to St. Louis.[47] There, after President Higbee helped people unload from the *Pride of the West,* his shepherding work apparently ended. Passenger Ballard noted that it was Elders Kelsey and Ross who chartered the *Saluda,* a vessel he called "another old worn out steam boat."[48]

Who Were the Passengers?

No passenger lists survive, so it is difficult to know precisely how many people were on board when the *Saluda* left St. Louis. But several contemporary estimates did get recorded. It's clear that not all the Mormons who came upriver from New Orleans became *Saluda* passengers. Some stopped in the St. Louis area to work. Others needed more time in the city to take care of personal matters or for health reasons but went upriver a few days after the *Saluda.* Many Mormons who were not on the *Kennebec* were already in the city, intending to go to Kanesville; some of these boarded the *Saluda,* while others, such as Abraham O. Smoot, waited for a better boat (as mentioned in chapter one).

On March 30, 1852, the *Missouri [Daily] Republican* published a list of "Steamboats Advertised to Leave This Day." Last on its list was the *Saluda,* to leave at noon for Kanesville (Council Bluffs). "On the thirtieth of March she sailed from St. Louis, with about one hundred and seventy-five persons on board," LDS historian Andrew Jenson calculated, of whom about ninety were church members, including a number of the passengers who had crossed the Atlantic in the *Kennebec.* There were also on board some church members from St. Louis and others from the state of Mississippi.[49] A Mormon in St. Louis named Wrigley told the *Missouri [Daily] Republican* that the *Saluda* started out with "a large crowd of cabin passengers," including "some outward bound Californians." In addition to the cabin passengers, the "principal portion of her deck passengers were Mormons." How many? Seventy, Elder Wrigley said—forty-five who had been on the *Kennebec* and twenty-five in Mormon families from Mississippi.[50] President Higbee, who didn't go on the *Saluda* but stayed in St. Louis to purchase cattle for wagon trains near Kanesville, noted on March 30 that "about 100" Mormons went on the *Saluda.*[51] Abraham O. Smoot estimated on April 14 that about 115 Mormons got on board in St. Louis and that there were about 175 total passengers at

---

[47]   Dean L. McLeod, "James Ross: The Experiences of a Scottish Immigrant to America," *Family Heritage* 1 (December 1978): 178–79.

[48]   Reminiscences and Diary of Henry Ballard, March 14, 1852, LDS Church Archives.

[49]   Andrew Jenson, "Church Emigration," *Contributor* 12 (July 1892): 408–14.

[50]   "Another Terrible Steamboat Explosion," *Missouri [Daily] Republican,* April 10, 1852, 2.

[51]   Reminiscences and Diaries of John Sommers Higbee, March 30, 1852. Higbee wrote on April 9 that he received money to purchase cattle for a Sister Yates. On April 10–12, 1852, he made additional preparations to go west with the Saints. On April 13, 1852, he wrote, "Got on the 'Delaware' steamer. Two days later (April 15, 1852) he noted, "Started in company with Brother [John] Pack & [John] Spiers & about 30 more Saints & about 400 gold seekers with 40 wagons & about the same number of horses & mules."

[52]   Abraham O. Smoot to Brigham Young, April 14, 1852, Incoming Correspondence, Brigham Young Papers, LDS Church Archives.

the time of the explosion.[52]

Because Higbee and Smoot were in the best positions to know, their statements are likely the most accurate indication that between 100 and 115 Mormons were aboard. Not all of them reached Lexington, however; about a dozen left the *Saluda* part way to Lexington, leaving about ninety on board when the boat reached Lexington.

In addition to the Mormon group, historian Dan Spies points out, "there were also other immigrants bound for California and Oregon and a number of other passengers bound for intermediate points on the Missouri."[53] One *Saluda* survivor, Colonel Holmes of Sullivan, Wisconsin, reported that when the steamer left St. Louis, it had nearly four hundred passengers. He recalled that there were "a great many California emigrants, and a body of the Mormons."[54] However, his estimate appears to be inflated.

How many non-Mormon passengers started out and how many disembarked along the way cannot be exactly determined. At the time of the explosion, about eighty-five were still on board, in addition to about ninety Mormons.[55]

Captain Belt and His Crew

One day after the *Saluda* exploded, the St. Louis *Missouri Republican* published a list of the steamboat's officers, as follows:[56]

Captain	Francis T. Belt
First Clerk	Capt. F.C. Brockman
Second Clerk	Jonathan Blackburn
First Pilot	Charles La Barge
Second Pilot	Louis Guerette
Engineer	Josiah Clansey
Engineer	John Evans
Mate	William Hemler [Hendley]
Watchman	John Conner
Bar Keeper	Peter Conrad

Captain Belt, age thirty-five, was part owner and master of the *Saluda*. He had spent a lifetime on the river and was considered an "experienced boatman" who was "well known on the rivers as an able commander, and was endeared to all who knew him for his kindness and generosity."[57]

Like Captain Belt, both of the *Saluda*'s pilots were men with good river expertise. First pilot Charles La Barge grew up in the St. Louis area and was, in fact, from one of the oldest families in St. Louis. Charles had six siblings,

---

[53] Dan Spies, "The Story of the Saluda," unpublished paper from the University of Missouri Arts and Science papers, 1908–65, no. 3406. It is housed at the University of Missouri at Columbia.

[54] "Steam Boat Explosion," *St. Joseph Gazette,* April 14, 1852, 2.

[55] Jenson, "Fifty-sixth Company," 408. These two figures total 175 passengers. This is the precise number used by Smoot, as noted above, which Jenson probably used to derive his estimate.

[56] *Missouri Republican,* April 10, 1852.

[57] "Died," *Missouri Republican,* April 12, 1852, 2.

one of whom was Joseph La Barge Jr., a steamboat captain well known in Missouri River history.[58] Charles gained his initial expertise as a pilot from his brother Joseph. Second pilot on the *Saluda*, Louis Guerette, was a brother of Charles La Barge's wife.[59] Pilots, it was said, were the kings of the river and were entitled to a substantial wage for their skilled services:[60]

> Piloting on the Missouri was a science, and the skillful pilot, was a man of wonderful memory of localities. No man, indeed, ever became a first-class pilot who was not endowed with this peculiar faculty. He was required to know the river throughout his entire run as a schoolboy knows the path to the school house. He had to know it throughly, upside down, endways, inside, outside, and crossways. He had to know it at midnight of the darkest night—when called on watch—as well as in daylight. He was expected to know every sandbar, every crossing, chute, towhead and cutoff; the location of every wreck and every dangerous snag, from one end of the river to the other. He had also to be able to determine the location of the boat on the darkest night from the reverberation of the sound of the whistle, as the echo resounded from the adjacent bluffs. He was expected to know every landmark on the shore, the location of every cabin, and the peculiar bark of every squatter's dog.[61]

First clerk, Captain F. C. Brockman, was the boat's agent responsible for its passenger lists, ticket sales, accounting, and money. He is one of three known officers who survived the explosion. The others were William Hemler [Hendley, Emory, Emery], mate and Peter Conrad, listed as bar-keeper, who was half-owner of the *Saluda,* with Captain Belt.[62]

Altogether, counting passengers, officers and crew, it appears the *Saluda* was carrying probably between 200 to 250 people when she shoved away from the St. Louis wharf on March 30 and nosed northward up the Mississippi River, heading for the mouth of the Missouri River twenty miles away.

To date, name lists of those on the *Saluda* have been sketchy. In Appendix B, based on new research we have identified by name 172 of the passengers, officers and crew. This is the most complete list yet assembled of *Saluda* personnel.

---

[58] Hiram Martin Chittenden, *History of the Early Steamboat Navigation on the Missouri River Life and Adventures of Joseph La Barge* (Minneapolis, Minnesota: Ross & Haines, Inc., 1962), 13.

[59] Chittenden, *History of the Early Steamboat Navigation,* 124.

[60] According to Chappell, *A History of the Missouri River,* 83, the mariners' wages were gauged by the labor, risk, and earnings from the river business. "Captains received from $250 to $300 per month, clerks from $125 to $250, mates from $100 to $250, engineers about the same as mates. Of course these wages included board." Yet Chappell points out that "it was the pilot however, who divided the profits with the owner, and sometimes received the larger share. He was the autocrat of the boat and absolutely controlled her navigation."

[61] Chappell, *A History of the Missouri River,* 83.

[62] *Missouri [Daily] Republican,* April 10, 1852, 2; April 17, 1852, 2, notes the names of these officers who survived. William Hemler is also noted in the April 17, 1852 reference as "W. Hendley."

CHAPTER THREE

Upriver Push
to Lexington

Instantly a Negro drayman . . . lifts up the cry, "S-t-e-a-m-b-o-a-t a-comin!"
. . . The town drunkard stirs, the clerks wake up, a furious clatter of drays
follows, every house and store pours out a human contribution, and all
in a twinkling the dead town is alive and moving. Drays, carts, men,
boys, all go hurrying from many quarters to a common center, the wharf.
. . . And the boat is rather a handsome sight, too. She is long and sharp
and trim and pretty; she has two tall, fancy-topped chimneys, with a
gilded device of some kind swung between them; a fanciful pilothouse,
all glass and "gingerbread," perched on top of the "texas" deck behind
them; the paddle boxes are gorgeous with a picture or with gilded rays
above the boat's name; the boiler deck, the hurricane deck, and the texas
deck are fence and ornamented with clean white railings; there is a flag
gallantly flying from the jack-staff; the furnace doors are open and the
fires glaring bravely; the upper decks are black with passengers; the
captain stands by the big bell, calm, imposing, the envy of all; great
volumes of the blackest smoke are rolling and tumbling out of the
chimneys—a husbanded grandeur created with a bit of pitch pine just
before arriving at a town . . . the captain lifts his hand, a bell rings, the
wheels stop; then they turn back, churning the water to foam, and the
steamer is at rest.[63]

   Costs for a passenger ticket depended on how far up the river a passenger
wanted to go. In 1848, one group of Mormon emigrants paid an adult fare of
$5 each to steam up the Missouri River from St. Louis to the Council Bluffs,
area.[64] A few collections of old steamboat tickets survive, including one in
Lexington.[65] Printed on the ticket's back was a list of towns along the river
and mileages from St. Louis—and for some reason the mileage figures varied

---

[63] Mark Twain, *Life on the Mississippi,* 33–34.

[64] Sonne, *Saints on the Seas,* 99. This should be compared with modern-day currency. According to Samuel
Clark (research assistant for author Hartley), "Dollar Calculations Information Sheet," typescript, 5pp., in
authors' file, in 1852, the dollar value was about twenty-two times less than it is today. Thus, a $5 fare would
be the equivalent of about $110 in the year 2000.

[65] In the museum at the Battle of Lexington State Historic Site.

a bit from one steamboat company to another. Here are some of the towns and distances listed for a trip from St. Louis to Kanesville (Council Bluffs) on the steamboat *Sam Gaty*'s ticket:

Mouth Missouri River	20
St. Charles	45
Augusta	76
Washington	84
Portland	141
Jefferson City	174
Rocheport	217
Boonville	227
Arrow Rock	241
Glasgow	257
Cambridge	267
Brunswick	292
Waverly	346
Lexington	372
Sibley	408
Liberty	427
Kansas [City]	457
Leavenworth [Kansas Territory]	496
Weston	504
St. Joseph	566
Iowa Point	606
Council Bluffs [Kanesville] Iowa	783

For *Saluda* passengers going to Kanesville, most of whom were the Mormons on board, the journey normally took ten days, depending on river conditions and the steamboat's performance.

Dangerous and Difficult River

The "Big Muddy," named such for the churning currents that muddied its waters, is America's longest river and its most difficult to harness.[66] To make that point, historian Rudolph J. Gerber half jested that "of all the variable things in creation, the most uncertain of all are the actions of a jury, the state of a woman's mind, and the condition of the Missouri River."[67] While Mark Twain's Mississippi River required professional pilots who knew the river, the Missouri River boatmen bragged that "boys could navigate the Mississippi, but the Missouri demanded men."

---

[66] Michael Gillespie, *Wild River, Wooden Boats: True Stories of Steamboating and the Missouri River* (Stoddard, WI: Heritage Press, 2000), 37 notes that 1861 US Army topographical engineers set the length of the Missouri River at 2,824 miles, which would make it the longest river in North America. Chappell, *A History of the Missouri River*, 1, puts the length of the river at 2,546 miles.

[67] Rudolph J. Gerber, "Old Woman River," *Missouri Historical Review* 56, no.4 (July 1962): 328.

Historian Phil E. Chappell observed the progressive navigation history of the "Big Muddy":

> The first navigator of the Missouri River was the little blue-winged teal; the next, the Indian with his canoe; then came the half-civilized French Canadian voyageur, with his pirogue, paddling up-stream or cordelling around the swift points. At a later day came the fur-trader, with his keel-boat; and still later, with the advent of steam engines, there came up the little "dingy,"—the single-engine, one-boiler steamboat. At last the evolution was complete and there came the magnificent passenger steamer of the '50s—the floating palace of the palmy days of steamboating.[68]

The decade of the 1850s is referred to as the "golden era" of steamboating.[69] But even if they were elaborate steamers, they still frequently encountered a hostile river. No matter the craft, dangers were ever-present. Father Pierre-Jean DeSmet, a Jesuit missionary and earlier traveler on the Missouri, offered a warning based on his firsthand experiences: "I will remind you that steam navigation on the Missouri is one of the most dangerous things a man can undertake. I fear the sea, but all the storms and other unpleasant things I have experienced in four different ocean voyages did not inspire me with so much terror as the navigation of the somber, treacherous, muddy Missouri."[70]

Of great danger, Father Desmet warned, were snags lurking in the water that, if hit, could puncture a hull and sink a boat in minutes. The river, he said, "has the appearance of a whole forest, swallowed up by the immense river. Gigantic trees stretch their naked and menacing limbs on all sides; you see them thrashing in the water, throwing up foam with a furious hissing sound as they struggle against the rapid torrent."[71] Churning and fast flowing, the Missouri cuts away banks and shorelines, shifting its course year by year. It is said that Missouri farmers who had fields near its banks would "often harvest catfish and driftwood instead of corn and wheat."[72]

Snags sank many steamboats, sending valuable cargoes into the deep and drowning hundreds of passengers and crews. One official count says that between 1819 and 1897, 289 steamboats sank in the Missouri. Of those, 204 had run aground or collided with snags or rocks. Other estimates say as many as 400 steamboats went down.[73]

---

[68] Chappell, *A History of the Missouri River*, 81.

[69] Chappell, *A History of the Missouri River*, 80.

[70] Gillespie, *Wild River, Wooden Boats*, 44.

[71] Gillespie, *Wild River, Wooden Boats*, 47.

[72] Gerber, "Old Woman River," 328.

[73] Gillespie, *Wild River, Wooden Boats*, 85. This appears to be a conservative estimate. Rudolph J. Gerber, "Old Woman River," 339, asserts that between 1819 to 1880, at least 450 steamboats worth a value of $10 million sank in the Missouri River. Chappell, *A History of the Missouri River*, 89, points out that three fourths of the steamboat wrecks on the Missouri in the nineteenth century took place between Kansas City and the mouth of the river; therefore, he refers to this segment of the Missouri as a "marine grave-yard."

Steamboats faced dangers other than snags. They could become stranded in low water, be pounded or stopped by ice jams, collide with other boats or floating debris, catch fire, and—most frightening of all—have their boilers explode.[74] "By far the deadliest risk in steam boating was the boiler explosion," steamboat historian Michael Gillespie observed. "Crude and imprecise methods of determining boiler water level led to most of these 'burst ups.'" One newspaper tally, he said, identified twenty-seven boiler explosions that took place between 1834 and 1852 on America's rivers with a loss of life totaling 1,002.[75]

Missouri Steamboats

America's major rivers served as the interstate highways of the early and middle nineteenth century—until railroad tracks replaced them. Unlike roads and steel rails, rivers were already free and already built. Men of enterprise used rivers to make money by moving freight and passengers. During steamboating's golden years, many steamboat owners amassed fortunes. Potential high profits outweighed risks of the river. When California's gold rush started, passenger business escalated for steamboats running from St. Louis to ports near overland trail outfitting centers, such as Independence, Kansas City, Weston, St. Joseph, and Kanesville/Council Bluffs. Likewise, the annual immigration of Mormon converts to Utah significantly boosted the passenger business. Famous Missouri river pilot Joseph La Barge "found that doing business with the Mormons was so profitable that for two years he never went north of Council Bluffs."[76]

Many steamboats became "packet boats," which meant they made regularly scheduled runs up and down the river. By the 1850s, townsmen and fishermen regularly saw riverboats pass up and down the Missouri bearing names like the *Ben Bolt, Clara, F. X Aubrey,* and *Arabia.* The cry of the steamboat whistle became a familiar and welcome sound along the river.

Steamboats were either stern-wheelers or side-wheelers. Side-wheelers were faster and more maneuverable because one paddle could go in reverse while the other went forward, thereby quickly turning the vessel. In 1851 Jean Rio Griffiths, an emigrant from England, penned a detailed description of the steamboat *Concordia* on which she rode from New Orleans to St. Louis. While the *Concordia* was twice the size of the *Saluda,* her word picture helps visualize the sections and features of a steamboat:

> The engines and boilers are on the deck, the stoke-hole quite
> open on each side and the firemen have an uninterrupted view

---

[74] For a detailed discussion of the causes of steamboat accidents, see Louis C. Hunter, *Steamboats on the Western Rivers: An Economical and Technological History* (New York: Octagon Books, 1969), 271–304. This is generally considered to be the best source for a serious study of steamboating on the western rivers.

[75] Gillespie, *Wild River, Wooden Boats,* 87.

[76] Harry Sinclair Drago, *The Steamboaters: From the Early Side-wheelers to the Big Packets* (New York: Dodd, Mead and Company, 1967), 148.

of the country. . . . There is a clear passage of 8 feet in width all round the boat, except where it is stopped by the paddle boxes, and those have got steps both up and down; from this which is called the lower deck you ascend by a handsome flight of steps to what is called the Hurricane deck, which is an open gallery 5 feet wide, entirely round the vessel with a low railing next to the water and roofed overhead, there are chairs here, for the accommodation of the passengers. On the inner side of this gallery is a row of cabins with 2 doors each, one opening on to the gallery, the other into the Saloon. . . . Here the cabin passengers dine, etc. The ladies cabin is placed astern . . . and is splendidly furnished with sofas, rocking chairs, work tables and a piano. The floor, as well as the saloon's, is covered with . . . carpeting. There is also a smoking room for the gentlemen, opening out of the saloon in which are card-tables etc. In front of this there is a large open space, the whole width of the ship roofed over like the gallery and furnished with seats.

From this is another staircase, ascending to the upper deck, on which are built several neat cabins for the officers. The one forward encloses the steering wheel. Here stands the pilot, completely secured from wind and weather. To the wheel two ropes are attached which are conveyed downward to the lower deck, each rope is then fixed to a lever, which works the rudder, the whole arrangement is very simple, and the elevated position of the pilot, 40 feet above the lower deck, enables him to see and avoid any collision with snags, which are pretty plentiful. . . . The tops of the two funnels are 10 feet higher [than the upper deck], they are placed forward and when there is a head wind, the upper deck is covered with hot cinders. They burn wood, not coal, and when the steam gets low, or they want to pass a steamer in advance of them, the firemen throw on rosin by shovelfuls.[77]

In the Eastern United States, steamboats mainly carried freight. But western ones, with rare exceptions, carried both freight and passengers. While freight traffic was financially much more important, few owners resisted the potential extra income from the relatively higher rates and light weight of the passenger trade. As a result, it is the glamour and romance of the passenger aspect of steamboats that captures imaginations, not the hauling of freight.

The steamboats brought together western farmers, southern planters, merchants, politicians, artists, theatrical companies, titled Europeans, writers, speculators, preachers, slave traders, and gamblers—the rich and not so rich (not the poor; they were on the main deck) in a grand social mix. To an extent, social barriers were lowered and horizons broadened. In the evenings,

---

[77] Jean Rio Griffiths Baker Diary, March 29, 1851.

passengers shared the folk music of the black deck crews. They learned something of the art of the river piloting—and listened to tall tales spun that were altogether too difficult to swallow. On boats with adventurous captains, lucky passengers delighted in the thrills of the impromptu races that enlivened the river scene.[78] Michael Gillespie explains that cabin passengers could enjoy plentiful meals in the main cabin as well as service from chambermaids and stewards in their own stateroom. On the other hand deck passengers had to finance their own meals, had no service, no privacy, and were crowded by freight, filth and awful smells. The customer ratio was estimated at about one cabin passenger to three or four deck passengers.[79]

The *Saluda*

By 1852, the *Saluda* had a checkered history. Her hull was built in 1846 in Cincinnati, Ohio, and then towed to St. Louis that April. On April 28, workmen installed in her the boilers and engines taken three months earlier from a sunken year-old Mississippi steamer, the *Windsor*. Captain William H. Boyce, owner and master of the sunken *Windsor*, acquired the new hull from Cincinnati and apparently named it *Saluda*.[80] She was first registered, giving her a legal right to be in business, on June 1, 1846.[81] Licensing records say she was 177 feet long and 25 feet wide and weighed 223 tons. When she was launched, one reporter judged her to be an impressive steamboat (and gave more precise measurements of her size):

> This fine new steamer made her trial trip last Saturday, with a large party of ladies and gentlemen on board; and in her per-formance fully equaled the highest expectations of her owners, and added further testimony to the skill of St. Louis mechanics. She is a beautiful craft, 162 feet on the deck, 179 feet beam, 26 feet 8 inches in breadth, 24 feet 6 inches floor, and 5 1/2 feet depth of hold. She has two boilers 30 feet in length, and 2 engines, cylinders 17 inches in diameter, with 7 1/2 feet stroke; her [paddle] wheels are 20 feet in diameter, with 10 feet buckets. Her gentlemanly commander, Capt. Wm. Boyce, designs running her in the Missouri river trade; and to our friends above we recommend her as a fine specimen of river craft, commanded by skillful and accommodating officers.[82]

---

[78] Primm, *Lion of the Valley*, 162–63.

[79] Gillespie, *Wild River, Wooden Boats*, 25–26.

[80] [St. Louis] *Missouri Reporter*, April 29, 1846, 3.

[81] St. Louis steamboat enrollment, on microfilm titled "Vessel documentation Records from the Port of St. Louis, 1835–1944. Copies of licenses of vessels over 20 tons. Volumes B64–B66." These enrollments are located in the Ruth Ferris Collection of the Herman T. Pott National Inland Waterways Library, a special library within the Mercantile Library at the University of Missouri-St. Louis. Appreciation is extended to Bette Gorden, curator of the Herman T. Pott Waterways National Inland Waterways Library, for bringing this to our attention.

[82] "The Saluda" *St. Louis Weekly Reveille*, June 8, 1846, 884.

Near the end of her first year, on March 6, 1847, an advertisement in the *St. Louis Daily Union* claimed the *Saluda* was "not surpassed by any boat on the river."[83]

But before it turned two, the unpredictable river claimed it. In the fall of 1847, the *Saluda* struck a snag near Rocheport, midway across Missouri, and sank. Submerged for several months, a sandbar formed around her. Owner Boyce sold it, where it lay, to a Boonville resident. The man, whose name is not recorded, dug the *Saluda* out, refloated it "as good as ever," and salvaged and sold its cargo of hemp and other goods for $800. He brought the *Saluda* down to St. Louis where it was cleaned and repaired. By February 1848, it was back in service, still powered by her original two boilers and two engines.[84]

On August 4, 1849, George Kingsland licensed the *Saluda,* listing his name as "master and sole owner." The *Saluda's* August 30, 1851, registration shows that Peter Conrad was the sole owner and master.[85] On March 10, 1852, the *Missouri Republican* reported that Captain Francis T. Belt had purchased half of the *Saluda* three weeks earlier for $1,200, and Peter Conrad continued to own the other half. By then she was considered an old steamboat. "In 1850, the natural life span of a Mississippi sidewheeler was considered to be five years," one expert calculated, "but a Missouri River boat had only a three-year life expectancy because of the greater hazards on that tempestuous stream."[86]

Current Events

No year saw greater overland trail traffic to the West Coast and to Utah than 1852, which meant that steamboat traffic likewise ran heavy that year. In addition to increased westward emigration, history books list several other happenings of historical importance that year. United States President Millard Fillmore was serving his last year in office. Author Harriet Beecher Stowe published her novel, *Uncle Tom's Cabin,* which quickly fanned antislavery coals into a burning flame. The first through-railroad train from the East Coast reached Chicago in February. The Wells Fargo Company was founded in New York, and the business partnership of Anheuser and Busch commenced in St. Louis.[87]

Steaming to Lexington

After the *Saluda* left St. Louis on March 30, it churned up the Mississippi River for twenty miles, turned into the mouth of the Missouri River, and headed

---

[83] *St. Louis Daily Union,* March 6 1847, 3.

[84] *The Missouri Statesman,* February 25, 1848; *Lloyd's Steamboat Directory* (1856); W. J. MacDonald, "The Missouri River and Its Victims: Third Article," *Missouri Historical Review* 21, no. 4 (July 1927): 593.

[85] St. Louis steamboat enrollment, on microfilm titled, "Vessel documentation Records from the Port of St. Louis, 1835–1944," Mercantile Library, University of Missouri-St. Louis.

[86] Primm, *Lion of the Valley,* 163.

[87] James Trager, *The People's Chronology: A Year-by-Year Record of Human Events from Prehistory to the Present,* rev. and updated (New York: Henry Holt and Company, 1992), 458–61.

up that more turbid, yellowish watercourse, a route Captain Belt was quite familiar with. Concerning this route, one traveler wrote on April 29, 1852:

> Everything was new and strange: the low lands and dark, dismal forest had but little charm to engage the passenger's attention, and if he took the river into consideration, a more unpleasant scene would be hard to contemplate. Drift wood, snags, sand bars, and the muddy, troubled water made up a picture long to be remembered by those who for the first time sailed upon this great river.[88]

During the next few days, the *Saluda* pushed against a swift current and dodged dangerous floes of ice. It passed the Missouri River towns of St. Charles, Washington, Herman, and Jefferson City, Missouri's state capital. She reached Rocheport—the site where she had sunk four-and-a-half years before. Then, she pushed on to Boonville.[89] Very likely the *Saluda* stopped at several of these towns that dotted the river to obtain needed wood for steam power.[90]

Passengers passed the time by watching the river and landscapes drift by, and by visiting. Possibly the *Saluda,* like other steamboats, had piano players and performers on board who provided some entertainment. Perhaps the *Saluda* passengers heard, at least once, Stephen Fosters' song, written in 1846, "Oh! Susannah," which by then had become the anthem of the Gold Rush.

On April 2, the *Saluda* reached Glasgow, and on that day or the next, she stopped at Brunswick, nearly three hundred miles from St. Louis and about eighty miles down river from Lexington.[91] Elder Kelsey had made preparations before leaving St. Louis to disembark at Brunswick to buy cattle and herd them overland to Kanesville. He left the boat, as did George May, his son James, Alexander and John Gillespie, and about eight others.[92] Possibly other *Saluda* passengers left the boat at Brunswick or at stops before Brunswick.

The Lexington Bend

On Sunday, April 4, Captain Belt spotted the town of Lexington looming ahead on the larboard side. His boat had done well, reaching Lexington in five days. The average time for steamboats to reach St. Joseph was six days, so he was about two days behind schedule.[93] He had done a good job getting the

---

[88] Louise Barry, ed., "Overland to the Gold Fields of California in 1852: the Journal of John Hawkins Clark," *The Kansas Historical Quarterly* 11 (August 1932), 231.

[89] These Missouri River towns are listed on a map housed at the Missouri State Historical Society, Columbia, Missouri, dated March 8, 1853.

[90] Michael Gillespie, *Wild River, Wooden Boats,* 32, notes, "'Wooding up' was often the highlight of the day on an otherwise dull stretch of river. A stop for wooding might take up to an hour and usually was performed twice a day. Passengers could go ashore to escape the confinement of the boat during a wooding stop, though often they would line the railings to watch the spectacle."

[91] *Northern Missouri Republican,* April 10, 1852.

[92] Reminiscences of James May, 11, LDS Church Archives, notes "E. B. Kelsey, my father, me and 10 others left the boat and went over land for the Bluffs." We estimated eight others, inasmuch as Alexander and John Gillespie were counted as two of the ten whom May refers to.

[93] The six-day average is cited in Walter Williams, ed., *A History of Northwest Missouri,* 3 vols. (Chicago: Lewis Publishing, 1915), 1:159.

Saluda that far, that fast, given the high water from spring runoff and the hazards posed by the floating ice. His eyes scanned the town perched high up on the bluffs, then to the right, down to a point from the bluffs that jutted out into the river, making the river bend its course. The Lexington Bend, as it was called, had such a strong current sweep around it that the *Saluda,* he knew, must keep to the right of the river's center and stay on the side across from Lexington. "Just above Lexington, the oncoming current rounded a sharp bend from the northwest," *Saluda* student Dan Spies explained. "Whipping around the point of this bend, the current created a treacherous 'cross-over' from the north bank to the south bank along the Lexington bluff. This was the Lexington bend, a well-known hazard to river men of the day."[94]

Diarist Henry Ballard, soon to survive the *Saluda's* explosion, noted the difficulty the bend caused Captain Belt:

> April 4, Sun. We reached Lexington, and the captain and firemen did their best to make headway at this point, where it ran very swift, and after trying several hours they gave it up and crossed on the other side of the river, where there were no houses and tied up the boat for the night.
>
> April 5. The river was floating full of ice, large blocks from two feet thick and two rods long and larger. So we could not move any for four days.
>
> April 8, Thursday morning we crossed back to Lexington. The ice was not floating quite so bad. It broke the paddle wheels some and they repaired them for starting next day.[95]

By then, Captain Belt had lost several days, and neither he nor his passengers were very happy about it. On Thursday, with the *Saluda* tied up at the wharf and being repaired, many passengers, their numbers not known, gave up, got off, and sought land transportation to their destinations. According to one passenger, "The conduct of the officers of the boat, fortunately, had driven the great body of cabin passengers from the boat before it left Lexington, and hence the sufferers were mainly confined to the Mormons and others occupying the decks."[96] Those who left would ever be thankful that they abandoned the doomed steamboat.

Sometime on Thursday, another steamboat, the *Isabel,* reached Lexington and stopped there until Friday. Its captain, William Miller, secured the *Isabel* to the wharf some hundred yards down river from the *Saluda,* probably to give the *Saluda* ample room when she pushed out into the strong current and perhaps drifted downstream a little before heading for the Lexington Bend. Mormon Abraham O. Smoot, soon to be an eyewitness of the *Saluda's* explosion, was on the *Isabel.* "I followed a few days afterwards [after the *Saluda*

---

[94]   Dan H. Spies, "The Story of the Saluda," 2.

[95]   Reminiscences of Diary of Henry Ballard, April 4, 5, and 8, 1852, LDS Church Archives.

[96]   "Steam Boat Explosion," *St. Joseph Gazette,* April 14, 1852, 2.

left St. Louis] on the Isabel and overtook the Saluda at Lexington, where she was stopped by the float-ice and unable to proceed farther," he said.[97]

Perhaps at Lexington, the Saluda's passengers and crew heard the news received in Lexington a day or two before by telegraph, that on April 3 the steamer Glencoe had blown up at St. Louis. It was nearing the wharf when her boilers burst, killing and wounding scores of people. On fire and adrift, she set seven flatboats on fire as she floated down river.[98]

The Dunbars' Last Chance

Ironically, while many were getting off the Saluda at Lexington, the four Dunbars finally got on board—a very unfortunate decision for them. William Dunbar's summary of what his family did after they missed the Saluda in St. Louis tells of the family's third and final opportunity to avoid tragedy:

> Two days after the departure of the Saluda from St. Louis. I and family took passage on a first class steamer with the understanding that her captain would stop and put us on board the "Saluda" whenever we should overtake her. The Saluda being a slow boat, we soon caught up with her, but at the point where we did so, the river was so full of ice, and the boats so far apart (being on opposite sides of the river), that our captain refused to cross over to make the promised transfer.

The Dunbars' unnamed steamboat made it past the Lexington Bend and continued upriver, which did not please Dunbar:

> After the two boats had passed and repassed each other several times, the vessel we were on continued up the river until we got to within a short distance of St. Joseph. By this time our boat was so badly damaged by the floating ice, that she was compelled to haul to, and the passengers were cooly invited to leave the vessel. They were consequently dumped off on the east side of the river. I, however, refused to leave the boat, insisting that the Captain should redeem his promise and put me and my family on board the Saluda. To this he finally consented, after which the boat was allowed to drift back to Lexington, where we in the evening of April 8, the day before the terrible catastrophe took place, boarded the Saluda, which had tied up at the port of Lexington, waiting for the ice to clear away.

For reasons of money or space availability, the Dunbars prepared to spend the night camped outdoors on the upper deck:

> When we got on board the Saluda, we found that her hold was already crowded with passengers, hence some of them were given the privilege to sleep on the upper deck, in front of the

---

[97] Jenson, "Fifty-sixth Company," 414.
[98] S & D Reflector, September 1975, 8.

cabin door, and they were actually making their beds on the flooring which covered the boiler. Heavy canvass called tarpaulin water-proof, was put up to protect passengers from the winds and cold. On this upper deck, right on top of the boiler, I also made my family bed.[99]

Early the next morning, Dunbar painfully discovered what a dreadful mistake his family had made when they spread out their bedding and made their makeshift tent above the deadly boiler.

[99] Jenson, "Fifty-sixth Company," 411–12.

CHAPTER FOUR

Explosion and Tragedy

Sweating firemen fed their furnaces to almost incandescent heat with pitch pine and sides of rancid bacon. Then, sometimes the water level in a boiler sagged below the danger point and the intolerable compression of steam drove out a rust-weakened patch of iron shell or a loose rivet with a sudden explosion like that of dynamite. The other racked boilers exploded in turn, sundering the timbers of the hull and shattering into toothpicks the cabin overhead.[100]

April 9, 1852 was Good Friday—a holy day commemorating the tragic day Jesus Christ was hanged on a cross and killed. Easter Sunday was two days away, the holy day celebrating Christ's victory over death and the future resurrection of the dead. Lexington's ministers were preparing for Easter services. As of 7:00 A.M. Good Friday morning, they had no idea their hardest church work that holy weekend would be performing a mass funeral and burial service on short notice.

The Community of Lexington

Most of Lexington's early settlers came from southern states and brought slaves and southern ways of life with them.[101] Early in the 1800s, Lexington grew into a regional center for business and culture. Settlement started in 1815, and a river ferry was established in 1819. In 1822, John Aull built a store and warehouse on the river front and established, with brothers James and Robert, a general trading business. In time, he opened branches in Independence, Liberty, and Richmond and became a highly respected merchant in the West.[102]

Lexington obtained town status in 1822 and became the county seat of Lillard County, then for Lafayette County when it was formed. By the 1820s, Lexington was an important link in the chain of "two-way international trade" involving America's heartland and the Sante Fe Trail—local tinware, tobacco, and whiskey being traded for Mexican silver, mules, and leather.

---

[100] Manly Wade Wellman, *Fastest on the River,* quoted in John Brunner, *The Great Steamboat Race,* 231.

[101] Katherine Wilson Sellers, *Historical Glimpses of Lexington* (Lexington: Lexington Library and Historical Association, 1980), 4.

Hemp, produced on plantations worked by slaves, became an important export, baled or wound into ropes. Tobacco, too, was a profitable crop in the county. Growth meant that by 1845, Lexington was Missouri's third-largest city, with 1,679 residents—St. Louis being the largest with 34,410; and Hannibal second, with 1,789. But by 1860, St. Joseph and Kansas City had more population than Lexington.[103]

By the 1840s, Lexington's river business had become brisk. Steamboats picked up hemp and dropped off miners and settlers heading for the American West. Local boys came to know all the steamboats by the sound of their whistles or paddle wheels. In the 1840s and 1850s, six or eight steamboats often were docked "Under the Hill," as the landing area by the river was termed.[104] At upper and lower landings, new arrivals could see warehouses, rope factories, a flour mill, coal mines, and a foundry. "It was a common sight," a local newspaper reported, "to see a line of wagons half a mile long . . . waiting for their time to move forward down Broadway to the warehouses." The main landing area was four hundred feet long. What was called the "lower landing" was at the foot of Tenth Street.[105] The loading docks on the river front "swarmed with negro deck hands."[106]

With prosperity came better development of the city—more streets, more brick homes, a newspaper in 1840, the present Greek revival courthouse in 1849, a bank, a Masonic college, schools, and substantial brick churches built by Baptists, Christians, Cumberland Presbyterians, Episcopalians, Methodists, and the Presbyterians. German immigrants provided carpenters, masons, and plasterers contributing to Lexington's building boom. They established creameries, canneries, flour mills, and grain elevators. At Lexington, William H. Russell teamed up with wholesaler and retailer William Bradford Waddell and others to develop a freighting company. In 1850, they merged their business with Alexander Majors of Kansas City. Soon, the firm of Russell, Majors and Waddell became a major transportation company in the American West, hauling for the army and carrying mail. In 1860, their firm started the Pony Express.[107]

Nine years after the *Saluda* disaster, Lexington became embroiled in Civil War conflicts. The community was split regarding which side to favor. In the Battle of Lexington in September 1861, twenty thousand Missouri State Guard troops crushed a garrison of three thousand federal troops. Soon, Union forces occupied Lexington for most of the Civil War period.[108]

---

[102] B. M. Little, *The National Old Trails Road and Part Played by Lexington in the Westward Movement* (N.P.: B. M. Little, 1928), unpaged.

[103] Roger Slusher, "Lexington: A Brief History," typescript, excerpt in authors' possession, 1; "Few Recall 'Under the Hill,'" *Lexington Advertiser-News,* July 7, 1972.

[104] "Few Recall 'Under the Hill.'"

[105] Slusher, "Lexington: A Brief History," 2; Sellers, *Historical Glimpses of Lexington,* 4.

[106] B. M. Little, *The National Old Trails Road,* unpaged.

[107] B. M. Little, *The National Old Trails Road,* unpaged.

[108] B. M. Little, *The National Old Trails Road,* unpaged.

Good Friday Morning

At 7 A.M. in the morning, a few people were up and about. Dawn's early, gray light showed that the trees along Lexington's streets were bare—not yet budding because spring was not warm enough yet.

One resident already up and walking about was Colonel James Hale. . . Out in the river, ice had stopped running. . . Captain Belt and the crew were readying the *Saluda* for departure. . .

Captain William B. Miller, on the *Isabel*, had intentionally docked a distance away from the *Saluda*. He knew she was old and had old boilers that might be dangerous, so he was waiting for her to leave before he unloaded his freight. . .[109]

Abraham O. Smoot, an *Isabel* passenger, had just visited the *Saluda* and was nearly back to his boat. . .[110]

On board the *Saluda*, passengers were starting to stir. . .

John Sargent, a Mormon convert from Newbury, Berkshire, England, had five children with him. A thirty-seven-year-old widower, he longed to reach Utah where he, a masonry contractor, hoped to help build the Salt Lake Temple. He had sold his business and home and had paid in advance for two wagons and four ox teams to use in crossing the plains. Around his waist he wore a belt in which he had hidden one-tenth of his money, which would be his temple donation. Sargent employed a woman named Matilda Wiseman to be the governess of his children, and she, also a Mormon, was helping the family make this trip. Before they reached Lexington, John had persuaded Matilda to become his bride and mother to his children. The ceremony was planned for Good Friday April 9 on board the *Saluda*. Matilda, age twenty-six, had just dressed in her wedding gown that morning. . .[111]

John Tillery Mitchell and wife Rebecca, from Chicksaw, Mississippi, had four small children with them. . .

Welsh converts William Rowland and wife Rachel Evans had sailed to New Orleans in 1849 and had been living in Council Bluffs. Apparently they were in Lexington to visit William's brother, who lived in Missouri. With them were his two children by his deceased wife and two by Rachel. They came aboard the *Saluda* to return to Council Bluffs. . .

Scottish shepherd Henry Ballard had two sheep dogs on board with him. He had just spent the night sleeping by the boilers. Nearby was James Molton. Because George May and son James had disembarked at Brunswick, Ballard had charge of helping the May family. Ballard had gotten up early, gone

---

[109] The *Liberty Weekly Tribune,* April 16, 1852, 1. Frederick Way Jr., comp., *Way's Packet Directory 1848–1994* (Athens, Ohio: Ohio University Press, 1994), 226 indicates that the *Isabel* was built in St. Louis in 1850 and weighed 326 tons. She usually ran the St. Louis to New Orleans route.

[110] Jenson, "Fifty-sixty Company," 414.

[111] According to a biographical sketch written by Beth Hutchings Callister, "The Story of Matilda Wiseman Hutchings," 1–2 (courtesy of her great grandson, Gene Hutchings).

ashore, and brought back some provisions for the May family. Back on board, he was in the act of taking a drink of coffee. . .[112]

William Dunbar arose quite early, too. He and friends David Ross and Duncan Campbell started to fix breakfast. They hung kettles on the stove to boil water. Helen Dunbar and the two children were just getting out of bed. William and his two friends "stepped outside of the space encircled by the tar canvass," and William told Helen he would be back for breakfast in a few minutes. "This was the last I ever said to my wife and children while they were alive. . ."[113]

Harry Brown, from Ohio, had wife Rhoda and four children with him. Two daughters were still in bed. Harry was holding their youngster and standing over the provision box, getting the lad something to eat. . .

Pilots Charles La Barge and Louis Guerette were in the pilot house at the wheel. . .

Mate William Hemler and eight or ten of the hands, some of them blacks, were on the larboard afterguard, starting to push the *Saluda* out into the stream, using long poles. . .

A Lexington butcher stood opposite the men with the poles, obeying the mate's order to untie the line holding the *Saluda* to the levee. . .

Mr. Taubman, a miller, was standing on the wharf, having just been paid for flour sold to the *Saluda*. . .[114]

Captain Belt was conversing with Mr. Blackburn, the second clerk, between the chimneys on the hurricane roof. Captain Belt's hand was on the bell. . .

In the captain's cabin, his yellow dog was chained to the *Saluda's* six-hundred-pound safe. . .

Mr. Brockman, the first clerk, had just been standing on the hurricane roof conversing with Captain Belt and Mr. Blackburn but had just walked toward the back of the boat. . .

Thomas Childers, a Scotsman, and a friend had just ordered a drink from the *Saluda's* second bartender, a man named Laynell. . .

Engineers Josiah Clancey and John Evans were feeding the fires beneath the boilers. . .

The Explosion

Captain Miller of the *Isabel* claims to have heard Captain Belt remark, "I will round that point this morning or blow this boat to hell."[115] Captain Belt ordered the fire boxes filled and steam pressure increased and gave the order for the ropes to be tossed off so the *Saluda* could ease back from the levee. At about 7:30 A.M., the boat's big black bell clanged twice. The engines started.

---

[112] Reminiscences and Diary of Henry Ballard, April 9, 1852, LDS Church Archives.

[113] Jenson, "Fifty-sixth Company," 412.

[114] Robert O. and Linda S. Day, "The Steamboat Saluda Disaster: An Overview," eight- page typescript, April 1992, 3.

[115] Williams, *History of Northwest Missouri*, 159.

For some reason, an engineer had allowed a boiler to get dry. With engines engaged, the pumps forced cold water into the red-hot boiler. Before the paddle wheels had made three revolutions and about thirty feet from shore, floating out stern first, the *Saluda* suddenly blew up. The port-side boiler exploded first and then the starboard boiler. "The noise of the explosion resembled the sharp report of thunder, and the houses of the city were shaken as if by the heavings of an earthquake," witnesses said.[116] "The hull disintegrated. Timbers, splinters, pieces of boilers, engine parts, fragmented chimneys, bales, freight, and bodies were propelled skyward. A blossom of steam, smoke, and flying objects filled the air."[117]

On the bluff overlooking the wharf, Colonel James Hale and others were watching to see if the *Saluda* would make it around the bend this time. When it blew up, they were horrified to watch two-thirds of the boat disintegrate into splinters, smoke, and flying debris. Also watching from the bluff top, George W. Gaunt saw pilots La Barge and Guerette propelled higher than he was and then fall into the river and sink. Eyewitnesses saw some bodies fly up on the bluff side, onto the wharf, and out into the river. Debris rained on some houses atop the bluff. Stunned by what he had just seen, Colonel Hale hurried down toward the wharf. He explained that the *Saluda* safe had been blown seventy yards from the blast and noted that there was still "chained to it a dead yellow spotted pointer dog." He also noted that he found "the dead body of a large man, lying with his face downward and limbs extended as if he had sailed through the air like a blue rock. Every thread of clothing had been blown off his body. A sheet was soon spread over him and he was identified as Captain Belt, commander of the boat."[118]

The *Saluda*'s iron safe, in which the boat's papers were kept was broken into pieces. Clerk Brockman, uninjured, salvaged what papers he could.

A house on the levee was struck when one flue of the boiler passed through it. Steamboat fragments flew in the air and a piece struck and killed the butcher who had just released the line of the *Saluda,* after supplying her with meat.[119]

Abraham Smoot, walking back to the *Isabel* from the *Saluda,* heard and felt the explosion and turning around saw the following:

> Bodies of many of the unfortunate passengers and various parts
> of the boat flying in the air in every direction. Fortunately for
> the Saints [Mormons] on board, they were mostly on the deck
> of the boat and pretty well towards the stern, and they conse-

---

116 "Awful Calamity: Explosion of the Steamer Saluda—130 Lives Lost!!" *Liberty Tribune,* April 16, 1852, 1.

117 Sonne, *Saints on the Seas,* 103.

118 William Young, *Young's History of Lafayette County Missouri,* 2 vols. (Indianapolis, Indiana: B. F. Bowen & Company, 1910), 1:394.

119 "Another Terrible Steamboat Explosion," *Weekly Missouri Statesman,* April 16, 1852, 3. This article indicates it was a brick house. However, Young, *History of Lafayette County Missouri,* 1:395, points out that it was "a cottonwood log house on the levee, owned by J. H. Graham."

quently fared better than those below, or on the forepart of the boat, which was blown entirely to pieces. . . . My own preservation I can only attribute to the providence of the Almighty, for if I had remained a moment on the wharf to see the boat start, as would have been very natural for a person to do, I would have been blown into eternity as those were who stood there. [120]

Some who landed in the river swam to shore, on both sides of the river. On the north shore, among those saved was a little child, whose parents had been killed and whom a Mr. Ball said he wanted to adopt as his own.[121] Crewmen from the *Isabel* rowed out in a skiff and plucked others from the swift, cold waters. Survivor Henry Ballard said very few were saved from the river.[122]

A man who reached the wharf five minutes after the explosion wrote a lengthy account of the disaster, which the *Liberty Tribune* published a week later. He seemed to have a good grasp of the facts:

> On the morning of the 9th inst. at half past seven o'clock the steamer *Saluda* blew up just as she was leaving the Lexington wharf, on her upward trip for Council Bluffs. She had on board a large number of passengers, most of whom were emigrants for Utah. She had been detained at our wharf for several days by the large quantities of ice. As she was preparing to get under way, both boilers exploded, and the fragments of the ill-fated vessel were thrown on the top of the bluff, and even into the heart of the city, four hundred yards from the scene of disaster. Scores of human beings were blown into the river, and against the bluff and houses.

Bystanders told him they saw people and boat fragments thrown almost to the opposite side of the river, which at that point was eight hundred yards wide. "Several of those who were thrown into the river were but little hurt, and with lusty sinews they buffeted the current and floating ice and swam ashore."

When the man reached the river, "the boat lay at the wharf of a miserable wreck in the act of sinking." He saw that "the mangled remains of human beings were scattered over the wharf and on the bluff; and human blood . . . mingled with the water of the Missouri river." It soon became clear that some people were trapped in the wreckage:

> Forward of the ladies cabin, and about two-thirds the length of the entire boat, the ill-fated *Saluda* lay a mass of ruins, beneath which were lying, men, women and children; some of whom were yet alive. Their groans, and shrieks and sobs, and the plaintive wailing of helpless babes carried grief and desolation

---

[120] Jenson, "Fifty-sixth Company," 414.

[121] *Richmond Herald*, April 16, 1852, 2.

[122] Reminiscences and Diary of Henry Ballard, April 9, 1852, LDS Church Archives.

to the hearts of those who were exerting themselves to relieve the suffers. The fountains of sympathy were broken up, and tears gushed forth from eyes which had not for years known weeping. Many brave hearts and willing hands were so unmanned as not to be able to lift a timber to disinter the living beings who were calling aloud for help.

He watched while "one pretty child, some two years old, was disinterred from the mass of ruins, unhurt. It stopped its plaintive cry and smiled when its mother hugged it to her breast." He somehow heard that the woman had lost three of her four children. Rescuers pulled a three-year-old from the wreckage "very slightly injured," who called for its mother and father.[123]

Very quickly, almost every able-bodied male in Lexington was at the levee, helping to remove bodies, pull out survivors, and search for the missing. Colonel Hale, an eye-witness, said that citizens placed mattresses on the ground upon which they put "twenty-two large healthy-looking Englishmen" whose faces were "perfectly red from severe scalds." He said "the air was hideous" with moans of the badly injured. When he walked past the place a half hour later, twelve of the men on the mattresses were dead, "caused by internal burning through inhaling steam."[124]

Thomas Coleman saw the explosion or arrived at the scene immediately afterward. Writing his father on April 14, he described the "dreadful scene" at the levee. Captain Belt "was a dreadful sight to look at." He heard that about 135 lost their lives. "When they got the wounded and dead all together it was distressing. Some would have no legs, others burnt badly and, such shrieking and groaning I never heard before."[125]

News reporter James W. Black, from the *Richmond Herald* newspaper, hurried for ten miles and crossed over to Lexington. There he found the shore "covered with the limbs and mangled bodies of the sufferers." The *Saluda's* second clerk, Jonathan Blackburn, he said, was "literally torn to pieces."[126]

A few days later, the *Lexington Express* tried to recapture for readers what the scene was like immediately following the explosion:

> Twenty-six mangled corpses collected together, and as many more with limbs broken, and torn off, and bodies badly scalded —wives and mothers frantic at the loss of husbands and children —husbands and bereaved orphans engaged in searching among the dead and dying for wives and parents—are scenes which we can neither behold nor describe; yet, such a scene was presented to the citizens of Lexington on Friday—Good Friday—a day

[123] "Awful Calamity: Explosion of the Steamer Saluda—130 Lives Lost!!" 1.

[124] Young, *Young's History of Lafayette County Missouri,* 1:394.

[125] Thomas Coleman to Dear Father, April 14, 1852, photocopy of holograph, Coleman- Hayter, Letters, 1840–1900, University of Missouri, Special Collections Library.

[126] *Richmond Herald,* April 16, 1852, 2.

forever memorable in the annals of Christianity as the day that witnessed the redemption of man from endless death.[127]

Victims' Stories[128]

The William Dunbar Family. The Scottish bagpiper whose family had eluded three chances to stay off the *Saluda* paid a terrible price for finally boarding her the day before:

> We were standing on the deck watching the labors of the crew in starting the boat, and I witnessed just two revolutions of the paddle wheels, when I remember nothing more till I found myself lying on the bank of the river within three yards of the water's edge, with my clothes drenching wet, and my head all covered with blood. I felt as if I was just waking up from a deep sleep. I am of the opinion that I was blown in to the river by the explosion, and subsequently pulled out by some rescuing party, who then left me, thinking I was dead, but I have never been told by any one how it really happened.

When he regained consciousness, he looked around and then began to search for his wife and two children:

> I . . . saw the mangled form of a child lying close by me. Recognizing its clothing I soon made the startling discovery that it was my own dear baby boy, whom I, a short time before, had seen in its mother's arms. I attempted to rise to go over to the spot where my dead child lay, but found myself unable to do so, and I now also noticed a sharp pain in my back, as my spine had been severely hurt by being thrown so violently into the river; from the effects of this I have suffered with pains in my back ever since.

Dunbar's attempts to rise attracted attention, and two men came to his assistance. They carried him to a neighboring store, which had been turned into a temporary hospital:

> I arrived at this place just in time to see my wife, who was lying on the floor, breathe her last. She had been cast on shore by the explosion, and carried to the store in a dying condition. My other child, a little girl about five years old, was lying in the same room, among the dead, her body so mangled that I could scarcely recognize her, that a lady survivor also claimed her as her child. I have on several occasions since reasoned on the possibility of my being mistaken in identifying as that of my child, and wondered if it could be possible that my little girl was

---

[127] "The Explosion of the Saluda," *Missouri [Daily] Republican,* April 17, 1852, 2; reprinted from the *Lexington Express* for the date of April 13, 1852.
[128] See Appendix for a list of passengers and victims.

Typical Steamboat
Deck Layout

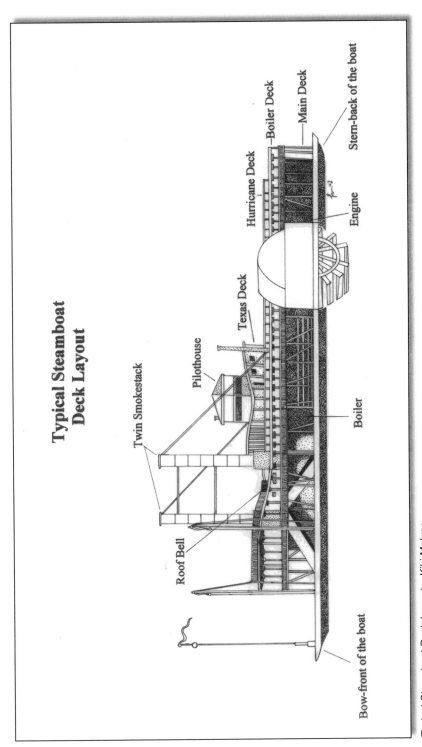

Typical Steamboat Deck Layout—*Kiki Melver*

Departure from Liverpool (1853)—*Frederick Piercy, Courtesy of LDS Church Archives*

New Orleans (1853)—*Frederick Piercy, Courtesy of LDS Church Archives*

St. Louis Levee—*Thomas Easterly, Courtesy of Missouri Historical Society*

St. Louis Levee—*Frederick Piercy, Courtesy of LDS Church Archives*

Back side of Omaha Steamboat Ticket—*Courtesy of Battle of Lexington State Historical Site*

Omaha Passenger Ticket—*Courtesy of Battle of Lexington State Historical Site*

"Steamer Omaha landing Mormons at Florence, Nebraska, in the Spring of 1854"— *George Simons, Courtesy of Council Bluffs Public Library*

Great Salt Lake City (1853)—*Frederick Piercy, Courtesy of LDS Church Archives*

Isabel Passenger Ticket—*Courtesy of Missouri State Historical Society*

Birds' Eye View of the City of Lexington - 1869—*Henry Beville, Courtesy of Library of Congress*

"Saluda at Dock"—*Linda Day, Courtesy of Lexington Historical Museum*

"Explosion of the Saluda"—*Terry McKee, Courtesy of Lafayette County Historical Society*

Dr. Edward G. Arnold House: Site of the Lexington makeshift hospital—*Courtesy of Brant and Michelle Neer, Lexington Heritage Tours*

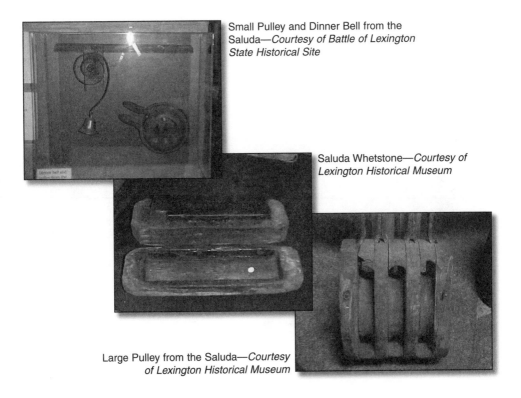

Small Pulley and Dinner Bell from the Saluda—*Courtesy of Battle of Lexington State Historical Site*

Saluda Whetstone—*Courtesy of Lexington Historical Museum*

Large Pulley from the Saluda—*Courtesy of Lexington Historical Museum*

Door of Saluda which was blown off at time of the explosion—*Courtesy of Lexington Historical Museum*

Franklin D. Richards: President of the British Mission and Emigration Agent At Liverpool in 1852—*Courtesy of LDS Church Archives*

John S. Higbee: LDS President of the Voyage of the Kennebec—*Courtesy of LDS Church Archives*

Eli B. Kelsey - Agent who charterted the Saluda steamboat at St. Louis—*Frank Esshom, Pioneers and Promient Men of Utah, 1913.*

James May: James got off the Saluda at Brunswick, Missouri, with his father George, Eli Kelsey, and 10 others to obtain cattle for crossing the plains. His father and mother both died of cholera on the journey. At that time he wrote, "Now there were 4 of us orphan children."—*Frank Esshom, Pioneers and Promient Men of Utah, 1913.*

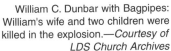

William C. Dunbar with Bagpipes: William's wife and two children were killed in the explosion.—*Courtesy of LDS Church Archives*

Abraham O. Smoot - Eyewitness of the Saluda explosion—*Courtesy of LDS Church Archives*

Henry Ballard: He had two sheep dogs on the Saluda which were lost.—*Frank Esshom, Pioneers and Promient Men of Utah, 1913.*

Louisa Sargent Harris: Louisa was only 10-years-old when she was burned in the explosion and a wagon wheel rolled over her head on the way to the Salt Lake Valley, but in both instances her life was spared.—*Courtesy of Lois B. Erickson*

Ellen [Sargent] Bremer with her daughter Lou Bodecker: Ellen was 12-years-old when she was orphaned after the Saluda explosion. Choosing to remain in Lexington, Ellen was adopted by a kind family, while her siblings continued to Salt Lake City and fulfilled their father's dream of gathering to Zion.—*Courtesy of Ruth M. White*

John & Sarah Ann [Sargent] Martin Family: Sarah was a 16-year-old survivor of the Saluda, and who later emigrated to Utah with some of her surviving siblings.— *Courtesy of Ruth M. White*

Rachel Evans: Rachel was 22-years-old when the Saluda exploded. Losing her husband, William, two children, and being left permanently crippled, Rachel did remarry James E. Harris and have eight additional children. She later died in 1918.—*Courtesy of Sherida Riggs*

Mary Roland [Rowland] James Riddle: She was severely burned in the explosion; Mary later married Thomas James in 1857 and Isaac Riddle in 1861 and raised several children. Born in 1838, died in 1920.—*Courtesy of Chauncey C. Riddle*

Sarah Brown Woodruff: She was 18-years-old at the time of the Saluda disaster. Sarah was struck in the head and left unconscious. Yet, she recovered. She married LDS Apostle Wilford Woodruff in 1853, who later become President of the LDS Church. When she died in 1909, she had eight children, 34 grandchildren and 24 great-grandchildren.— *Courtesy of the International Society Daughters of the Utah Pioneers.*

H. H. Gratz: H. H. Gratz was a Lexington citizen who served on a committee to raise money for the Saluda victims and who proposed that a committee be appointed to take charge of the orphans.—*Courtesy of Battle of Lexington State Historical Site*

John Spiers: About two weeks after the explosion, John Spiers visited the Lexington hospital to see the "badly scalded" victims of the Saluda.—*Orson F. Whitney, History of Utah, vol. 3, 1893.*

Matilda Wiseman was wearing a bridal gown, anticipating the hour of her wedding when the Saluda exploded, killing her fiance John Sargent.—*courtesy of Gene Hutchings.*

Co-author Fred E. Woods stands beside the Saluda Bell Monument in front of the First Christian Church in Savannah, MO. – *Courtesy of William G. Hartley*

Prince L. Hudgens: Hudgens was minister and organizer of the Savannah Christian Church; he purchased the Saluda bell for $17.50.—*Courtesy of First Christian Church in Savannah, Missouri*

Steven G. Wentworth, Lexington Public Administrator, leading citizen and founder of the Wentworth Academy—*William Young, Young's History of Lafayette County Missouri, vol. 2, 1910.*

Local Lexington historian, and Wentworth Academy instructor, Roger Slusher, stands near the site of the Saluda Explosion.—*Courtesy of William G. Hartley*

Captain Francis T. Belt: The Belt mounument in Lax Cemetery just northwest of Jerseyville, Illinois.—*Courtesy of Paul M. Hokanson*

Brant Neer, co-chairman of the Saluda 150 Committee and wife Michelle, owners of Lexington Heritage Tours.—*Photo courtesy Nola Whitely*

among those who fell into the hands of the special committee appointed by the citizens of Lexington to take care of the orphan children.[129]

David James Ross. David "was thrown into the middle of the river, and the current brought him near the shore some distance below, where somebody reached him a pole; and he was rescued."[130] David, survived the explosion, but he was injured. He managed to recover and go on to Salt Lake City later that year with his wife and two daughters.

The Duncan Campbell Family. Rescuers found Duncan Campbell's dead body "quite a ways down the stream." His wife and two of the children were killed, too. One son, Duncan Kelsey Campbell, slightly wounded, survived and was adopted by a Lexington family (see chapter five).

Henry Ballard. The Scottish shepherd was knocked unconscious and ended up inside the wrecked hull, without his dogs:

> I was blown about two rods and under a bunk with a man with his brains out. I was stunned and made senseless for about half an hour with a hole cut in my head near the brain. The sensation which I had while in this position was that I thought I was floating down the river upon broken pieces of plank. I finally saw daylight through a door way, which proved to be the door by the paddle wheels. A man ran past me and I followed him and jumped off on the side next to the land, which did not sink with me, but I could not stand after getting off. I had to lie down upon some boards laying there while the blood was streaming down my face from the wound in my head. I learned that none of the [May] family which I had charge of had been killed, but one somewhat wounded, which recovered.

When Ballard was "somewhat recovered," he tried to find his belongings. "I had two shepherd dogs on board from England, but they were blown away." He did find "the bread which I had in my hand, also my knife each covered with blood, and the tin cup that I had up to my mouth at the time, mashed flat as a dollar."[131]

The George May Family. Because the father, George, and son James had left the *Saluda* at Brunswick to help take cattle to Council Bluffs, friend Henry Ballard was helping care for seven other members of the May family. They all survived and left Lexington on the *Isabel.*[132]

The Harry Brown Family. Harry was traveling with his wife Rhoda and five children: Sarah, 18; Mary, 15; Ira, 13; Jane, 7; and son Edward, 2 1/2. Harry

---

129 Jenson, "Fifty-sixth Company," 412. Though Dunbar survived the explosion, while on a mission in England two years later, he noted that he was suffering from back pain which was a result of the *Saluda* accident. See "Journal History," September 26, 1854.

130 Jenson, "Fifty-sixth Company," 412.

131 Reminiscences and Diary of Henry Ballard, April 9, 1852, LDS Church Archives.

132 Reminiscences of James May, 10–13, LDS Church Archives.

was getting food from the provision box for the toddler when the boat exploded. They both were blown into a hole. Harry scrambled out of the mass of debris and found all his family, except the little one. Finally, Harry heard a voice call from below, saying, "Here I am, Papa." The child was pulled from the hole unhurt. Harry suffered internal injuries. Mother Rhoda was hit on her ear by a flying object. Daughter Sarah was struck on the forehead by something that knocked her out. The thirteen-year-old son, Ira, had his front teeth knocked out, his mouth badly cut, and his right leg broken.

When the Browns left Lexington on another boat on April 20, Harry became unconscious with brain fever and died on April 24. The surviving family stayed in Council Bluffs briefly and then left for Utah. Son Ira's leg did not heal, mortification set in, and all his toes dropped off during the trek to Utah. At Fort Laramie, his leg was amputated. Daughter Sarah reached Utah in 1851, but the rest of the family, because of Ira, did not arrive until 1852. One daughter, Mary, married in Wyoming and went to the Dakotas.[133]

Owen D. Harry. Owen was badly scalded, and his wife Emma was killed.

William Roberts Family. Out of William, his wife Selina, and five sons, only one son survived. Selina was badly injured and died three months later in St. Louis.[134]

The Rowland Family. A Rowland family story says that Captain Belt asked William Rowland, a Welsh boilermaker, to go down and examine one of the boilers to see if it was safe to put on more steam. Just as William said, "not another pound," as the story goes, the *Saluda* exploded and William was "blown to bits." Two of his children (Rachel and David) by his first wife, who was deceased, and the two born to him and his present wife Rachel in America (William and Sarah) were killed. This left Rebecca, whose leg was broken in two places, and her daughter Ann Eliza and stepdaughter Mary as the family's survivors. For the rest of her life, Rachel had a limp. Twelve-year-old Ann was adopted by a family going to California and was never heard from again.[135] Fourteen-year-old Mary suffered scalding burns on her shoulders, which scarred her for the rest of her life. In Utah, she married Thomas H. James, had two daughters, was widowed, and was remarried to Isaac Riddle.[136]

The John Tillery Mitchell Family from Chicksaw, Mississippi. Three of the four Mitchell children, from Chicksaw, Mississippi, died: Preston, age 2; William, 4; and Josephine, 6. John lost his legs because of the accident and died shortly afterward, probably in Council Bluffs.

---

[133] Sylvia Moses Handly Krause, "Sarah Brown Woodruff," typescript, February 1941, p. 1.

[134] Ruth M. White's *Saluda* file, Ogden, Utah.

[135] Hattie E. Walton Heninger, compiler-genealogist, *A Brief Historical and Genealogical Account of the Walton Family in the New England States, and Canada with Notes on Some of the Allied Families* (Salt Lake City: Hattie E. Walton, 1971), 56–57, The Church of Jesus Christ of Latter-day Saints, Salt Lake City, Church History Library.

[136] Records sometimes spell the name Rollins or Rolands. William spelled his last name "Rowland," according to a copy of his signature in the possession of his descendant, Mary Roland Riddle. See Ruth M. White to Elder and Sister Robert O. Day, July 14, 1992, in Mrs. White's *Saluda* file, Ogden Utah.

George Whitehead Family. Apparently, the entire George Whitehead family was wiped out—George, his wife, his mother, and two children.

The Gillespies. Scotsman John Gillespie and his brother escaped injury. His brother's wife Agnes was badly injured. John left them in Lexington and continued his journey. His brother and wife went upriver later and joined the Eli Kelsey wagon train.[137]

The Adolphus Young Family. Adolphus, wife Rhoda, and six children all survived. However, while crossing Nebraska toward Utah, the father and two children died of cholera.[138]

The John Sargent Family. The John Sargent family story is one of the saddest of all the victims on the *Saluda*. Of John, his five children, and their governness Matilda Wiseman, the youngest son, Joseph, age seven or eight, was lost in the river. John was killed. His body was found on the riverbank, robbed of clothing, and his belt containing his temple money was missing. A kind family took in the other four Sargent children and offered to pay their way back to England, but they refused. Ellen, 12, opted to stay with a family in Lexington and was adopted by them (see chapter five). Louisa, age 10, was badly scalded on her legs. She and her sister, Sarah Ann, age 15, and brother, John Jr., age 17, headed for Utah in the Eli B. Kelsey company. One day while walking beside the wagon, Louisa's injured leg gave way, and she fell beneath the wagon. Before the driver could stop, the wheel was on her head. Her life was spared, but her jawbone was so broken that she never again opened her mouth wider than half an inch. Louisa and Sarah Ann both married and settled in Weber County, Utah. John Jr. went on to California.[139]

Matilda Wiseman. Dressed in her bridal gown, Matilda was thrown into the icy waters, but was miraculously rescued. She remembered nothing about the explosion. After being nursed by some kind citizens of Lexington, she arrived at the Salt Lake Valley several months later. Ironically, she again became governess to a widower and less than eight months after the *Saluda* disaster she married him.[140]

Thomas Childers. Amid the gruesomeness and tragedy, a hint of humor emerged. When rescuers pulled Thomas Childers from the river, the Scotsman, who was about to take a drink at the bar when the boat blew up, said he could not remember whether he drank the whiskey he had just ordered, but, being a Scotsman, he *did* recall that he had not paid for the drink! His partner, unnamed, and bartender Laynell both perished.[141]

---

[137] John Gillespie Autobiography, *Our Pioneer Heritage,* 19:416–17.

[138] Rhoda Byrne Jared Young, in Eleanor McAllister hall, comp., *The Book of Jared,* 1963, 34.

[139] Ruth McFarland White and Lois Belnap Erickson, "John Sargent and His Family or the Tale of Two Sisters," unpublished family history article in possession of the authors.

[140] Beth Hutchings Callister, "The Story of Matilda Wiseman Hutchings," 1–2, notes that the widower was William Willard Hutchings. William and Matilda made their home in Beaver, Utah, where they were members of the Reorganized Church of Jesus Christ of Latter Day Saints. Matilda died in Beaver, Utah, in 1903..

[141] Bill Dye and Dan Spies, "The Saluda Story—2: Explosion Turns Riverfront into Horror Scene," *Lexington Advertiser News,* April 9, 1962.

Loss of Personal Property

Most of the baggage belonging to the emigrants was destroyed, but some of the merchandise on board, packed in tight barrels, and some ironware were saved. John Bernhisel, writing to Brigham Young, noted there was insurance to cover a literary loss. He recorded, "There was a small parcel of books for the Utah Library on board the ill fated Saluda when her boilers exploded, but they were fully insured, and hence can be replaced without loss."[142] James May who had left the *Saluda* earlier, learned that "Eli B. [Kelsey] had several thousand dollars worth of merchandise on board." He also noted that "all the little we had was lost." His sister Elizabeth "saw what was going on, that is, every lady was saying [saving] something and every[thing] they could lay hands on, and she did the same. Twenty saucers want [was] as much as they lost, which was not much."[143] Henry Ballard lost "one box of clothing entirely and one box in the hold of the vessel amidst mud and water, which was taken out after, and got a few of the things, but mostly spoiled."[144] Scotsman John Gillespie lost his clothing and tools.[145] Adolphia and Rhoda Young lost "much property."[146]

The *Isabel's* Generous Offer

After the explosion, the Captain of the *Isabel* "made the noble offer to take us free to the Bluffs," said Henry Ballard. "I took the boat again very reluctantly with what I had upon my back, and another shirt and one sock with no hat on my head and not money to buy anything for myself or the family, but the Lord raised up kind friends that were strangers to me and gave me money to buy provisions for the family to last till we got to the Bluffs."[147]

The May family, whom Henry was helping, also went on the *Isabel*. How many others accepted Captain Miller's offer of free transportation is not known. When the *Isabel* left three hours after the *Saluda* disaster, no one listed who or how many from the *Saluda* were on board. This failing is one main reason why an accurate tally of casualties and survivors cannot be made.

Isabel passenger Abraham Smoot decided to stay in Lexington and help look after some of the wounded Mormons until they could leave.[148]

Newspaper Reports and Casualty Estimates

Any serious discussion of the *Saluda* disaster must address the questions of how many were killed? how many were lost and missing? and how many were wounded? In the dozens of accounts published about the *Saluda* since

---

[142] John M. Bernhisel to Brigham Young, June 8, 1852, Incoming Correspondence, Brigham Young Papers, LDS Church Archives.

[143] Reminiscences of James May, 11, LDS Church Archives.

[144] Reminiscences and Diary of Henry Ballard, April 9,1852, LDS Church Archives.

[145] John Gillespie Autobiography, *Our Pioneer Heritage,* 19:416–17.

[146] Rhoda Byrne Jared Young, in Hall, *The Book of Jared,* 34.

[147] Reminiscences and Diary of Henry Ballard, April 9, 1852, LDS Church Archives.

[148] Jenson, "Fifty-sixth Company, 414.

1852, the estimates regarding how many died vary wildly from two dozen to 200 or more. Who is to be believed? Historians use a rule of thumb which says that accounts written by first hand observers are more reliable than those told second hand and versions written closest to the time usually are more trustworthy than those written later. In essence, we must ask: who was in the best position to know?

First Clerk F. C. Brockman, whose official position necessitated that he have the best understanding of passenger numbers, said that at the time of the accident, 175 people were still on board and that he knew of only about fifty of those still living. He said twenty were injured, most of them dangerously so. Based on his calculations, which don't take into account that some survivors might have left Lexington immediately on their own, some reports said that the loss of life would not be less than 135—assuming that up to ten of the critically wounded would die.[149]

One hour after the explosion, the steamer *Clara* arrived at Lexington and docked for just over three hours. Officers reported that in Lexington, "the excitement was such as to render it utterly impossible to arrive at any correct idea of the number killed and wounded. In fact, taking the crew and passengers, the general impression is, that the number killed cannot fall short of one hundred souls. The books of the boat have been lost, and Mr. Brookman [Brockman], the head clerk, is now at Lexington, endeavoring to arrive at a correct estimate of all injured, as well as the names of each individual."[150]

On April 13, the *Lexington Express* estimated that "the number of killed and badly wounded is about one hundred."[151]

On April 14, Abraham O. Smoot, who had been assisting the wounded, reported to LDS Church President Brigham Young that "the nearest Estimate that can be made of the entire loss of life is about 75 souls out of 175 passengers. The capt. & pretty much all the Crew was lost & her entire Cargo of freight."[152] Col. Holmes of Sullivan Wisconsin, one of passengers on *Saluda*, estimated that about 100 were lost—3 or 4 cabin passengers, 28 on the boiler deck, and 20 to 30 on the main deck.[153]

Based on these statements, the safest statement seems to be that about 90–100 were killed or lost, out of 175 people on board, including the officers and crew. (See Appendix A: "A discussion of how many died as a result of the *Saluda* explosion.")

---

[149] "Awful Calamity: Explosion of the Steamer Saluda—130 Lives Lost!!," 1.

[150] "The Steamer Saluda," *Missouri [Daily] Republican,* April 12, 1852, 2.

[151] *Lexington Express,* April 13, 1852.

[152] Letter of Abraham O. Smoot to Brigham Young, April 14, 1852, LDS Church Archives. This letter is published in its entirety in "Terrible Accident-Explosion of the Steamer Saluda—Seventy-Five Lives Lost!" *Deseret News,* May 29, 1852, 3. Although death estimates vary, this seems to be the most accurate, as Smoot was not only reliable in character but also an eyewitness of the victims who acted officially on behalf of the Church in these tragic circumstances. For more information on his life, see Loretta D. Nixon and L. Douglas Smoot, *Abraham Owen Smoot: A Testament of His Life* (Provo, Utah: Brigham Young University Press, 1994).

[153] *St. Joseph Gazette,* April 14, 1852.

Blame

Captain Belt's infamous remarks about rounding the bend or blowing the boat to hell, supposedly made to Captain Miller of the *Isabel,* are so deeply imbedded in the *Saluda* story that the blame for the disaster will forever swirl around him. Josiah Clancey, the second engineer, was blown ashore. He lived long enough to admit that he was the cause of the explosion—that he had no water in the boilers and consequently no steam—but that he acted in obedience to Captain Belt's orders.[154]

However, Captain Belt's relative, Henry B. Belt, the sheriff of St. Louis County, sent notice to Missouri newspapers that the statements attributed to Captain Belt "are unfounded." Sheriff Belt had talked to individuals who heard the dying confession of the engineer. They said that Clancey, in his dying moments, blamed himself for the explosion. They heard him declare emphatically and remorsefully that he himself was the "murderer"—he used that expression—and that Captain Belt knew nothing whatever of the condition of the boilers. The sheriff-relative maintained that "In a fit of pique at some severe remarks made by the Captain about not having stemmed the current, he [Clancey] shut the water from the boilers, determined at all risks, to have a quantity of steam that would force the boat through." The sheriff said further that others who knew Captain Belt spoke of his "extreme caution and prudence, in matters of this sort, [which] amounted almost to a too great timidity."[155]

There can be little doubt that Captain Belt, in view of the days of delay adding up, was determined that morning to get past the bend and that he let his engineers know he expected them to create maximum steam power to do it. Very likely, too, he felt pressured by complaints from some of the cold and frustrated passengers.[156] To remove primary blame from Captain Belt seems a bit lenient, especially in light of the fact that he had been in command of the steamboat *Planter* that had exploded four years earlier.[157] As co-owner of the *Saluda,* he had serious economic reasons for getting up river.[158] Sadly, Belt atoned with his life for any poor judgment he exercised that morning. All facts considered, perhaps it was the Lexington Bend which might be blamed. It posed such a problem that years later engineers got rid of it and straightened out the Missouri River's course at that point.

---

[154] *Missouri Statesman,* April 16, 1852.

[155] "The Late Captain Belt and the Explosion of the Saluda," *Liberty Tribune,* April 23, 1852.

[156] Sonne, *Saints on the Seas,* 103–4.

[157] Way, *Way's Packet Directory,* 374, notes that the steamboat *Planter* was built in 1846. A year later, it was bought by Francis T. Belt and his brother Captain L. T. Belt. "On Jan. 5, 1848, she exploded the boilers while loading grain at Jones Ferry, Twelve Mile Island, on the Illinois River, demolishing the cabin. Five lives were lost. Capt. Francis T. Belt was in command at the time."

[158] "Another Terrible Steamboat Explosion," *Missouri [Daily] Republican,* April 10, 1852.

CHAPTER FIVE

Lexington's Compassion

Then shall the King say unto them on his right hand, Come, ye blessed of my Father, inherit the kingdom prepared for you from the foundation of the world: For I was an hungred, and ye gave me meat: I was thirsty, and ye gave me drink: I was a stranger, and ye took me in:

Naked, and ye clothed me: I was sick, and ye visited me: I was in prison, and ye came unto me.

Then shall the righteous answer him, saying, Lord, when saw we thee an hungered, and fed thee? or thirsty, and gave thee drink?

When saw we thee a stranger, and took thee in? Or naked, and clothed thee?

Or when saw we thee sick, or in prison, and came unto thee?

And the King shall answer and say unto them, Verily I say unto you, Inasmuch as ye have done it unto one of the least of these my brethren, ye have done it unto me.[159]

Time stood still that terrible Friday morning in Lexington. The tragedy of the *Saluda* preempted whatever plans the residents had for that Good Friday. The town council had no emergency plan for dealing with the likes of this catastrophe, but the people saw immediately they had to somehow respond. The dead and dying, the scalded and torn, the orphaned and shocked, all needed help. Individuals rushing to the wharf saw a dozen problems demanding immediate attention. Who should be in charge? What building could serve as a makeshift hospital? Who should ride to nearby towns to solicit doctors to render aid? Which women had nursing experience? Who would tend to the orphaned children? Did those killed have relatives with them on the *Saluda?* How many were missing and how should they be searched for? Whose wagons could be recruited to transport the dead? Where could the corpses be kept until burial? Where should the moneys and properties salvaged from the wreckage and the dead be stored? Who could gather donated clothes for the victims bereft of suitable clothing?

---

[159] King James Bible, Matthew 25:34–40.

Having to face challenges of this magnitude inspired the unprecedented cooperation and effort from the citizens of Lexington. They rose to the need and demonstrated heroic compassion and service.

Caring for the Injured

An immediate call for help went out to doctors living in the vicinity of Lexington. Dr. William P. Boulware of Lexington helped as did other doctors, including Dr. William M. Bowring and William Gordon who went to Lexington "to assist in caring for those injured in the explosion of the Steamboat *Saluda*," according to Dr. Bowring's diary entry for April 9.[160]

Within minutes of the explosion, someone designated a large brick building at the upper end of the levee to serve as an emergency hospital, where volunteers received the injured.[161] As mentioned in chapter four, when rescuers found William Dunbar too injured to walk, two men carried him to a "neighborhood store"—really a warehouse—that also served as a makeshift hospital. There he saw his wife on the floor take her last breath, and a little girl whom he believed was his daughter, lying mangled among the dead in that same room.[162] A report prepared that day said that "the hospital contains eleven males and three females, all wounded."[163] Dunbar did not stay there long, thanks to a caring resident, not named:

> I had been in the store only a short time when a gentleman brought a hack in which he took me to his private residence, where I was treated with much hospitality and kindness, although the man admitted that he was one of those who years ago had shouldered his gun to help drive the 'Mormons' out of Missouri. Owing to the injuries my back had sustained, I was unable to move for several days, but I finally got strong enough to walk about, when I was shown the spot where the earthly remains of my wife and children were laid to rest.

In a few days, Dunbar mended enough to leave on a steamboat. The day he left, he said, "a few of the sick and wounded still remained in Lexington."[164]

The *Lexington Express* published an "Extra" edition on April 13 in which were listed the names of those known to be dead, missing, and seriously injured.[165] By then, twenty-one bodies had been found. Two of those, Captain Belt and second clerk Jonathan Blackburn, had been sent down river to St. Louis for interment. The rest, apparently, were buried in Lexington (see

---

[160] Charles Ekin, ed., *Diary of a Town, Wellington, Missouri*, Diary of Dr. William M. Bowring, entry for April 9, 1852. A photocopy of the diary is in the Charles Bowring Collection, folder 1, at the Western Historical Manuscript Collection, Ellis Library, State Historical Society of Missouri, University of Missouri at Columbia.

[161] *Lexington Advertiser-News*, April 9, 1962.

[162] Jenson, "Fifty-sixth Company," 412–13.

[163] *Jefferson Inquirer*, April 17, 1852 (from a report dated April 9).

[164] Jenson, "Fifty-sixth Company," 413.

[165] *Lexington Express*, April 13, 1852.

below).Ten people were unaccounted for. Undoubtedly, recovery parties had searched in boats and along the shores, looking for bodies that might have washed up. But after the rescue efforts of that first day, records fail to note if any more deceased victims were found down river.

In the wounded category, the newspaper listed the following people who were unable to immediately resume their journeys (many of those injured in the blast had not stayed in Lexington but had moved on):

Thomas Huff	Slightly
John T. Mitchell	Left thigh amputated
Owen O. Harry	Dangerously
Wesley Pogue	Nose Broken
George Marr	Left arm amputated
Michael Ambuston	Slightly
Mrs. Agnes Gillespie	Face and neck badly scalded
Mrs Rachel Roland	Leg broken
Mrs. Sarah McKachie	Spine dangerously injured
McKachie child	Slightly
W. Hendley, mate	Slightly
Peter Conrad, part owner	Dangerously injured
Charles Evans, carpenter	Slightly
Frederick Shultz	Slightly
Anthony Perkinmeyer	Badly
D. J. Ross	Slightly
W. McGee	Slightly
W. C. Dunbar	Slightly
Duncan Campbell, child	Slightly
Colored fireman	Slightly

"The ladies of our city," the article continued, "were active in affording relief to the wounded females, laying out the dead, and securing protection for the children who were saved." Several of the severely injured were placed in eight private residences for personal care and nursing, which arrangements the newspaper also listed:

Mrs. Sarah McKachie	Professor Patterson
McKachie daughter, age 8	Mr. George Wilson
McKachie son, age 7	Mr. James Nichols
McKachie daughter, age 3	Mr. F. Zellers
Mrs. Agnes Gillespie	Dr. Peebles
Mrs Rowland	Mr. A. Huntsberry
Rowland daughter, age 5	Mr. John George
Duncan Campbell, age 2 or 3	Mr. Henry Smock

Not on this list for some reason is the name of Matilda Wiseman, the governness and anticipated bride of John Sargent.

Citizen Committees

Within hours of the explosion, a town meeting was called to organize the citizens to deal with the wounded and destitute.[166] The meeting, by vote, created four committees. The first, comprised of John S. Porter, John Williams, and H. H. Gratz, raised subscriptions to fund the relief effort. They were instructed to petition the city council for an appropriation for that purpose. A second committee, whose members were George Cox, W. N. Holton, and Silas Silver, took on the responsibility to see that the dead were buried properly.[167] As a third committee, James W. Wetzel, B. F. Wallace, and W. A. Powell were assigned to supervise the care of the injured. Three more men—George Wilson, Paul Reinhard, and Fred Zeiler—were appointed to take charge of the orphans. At the meeting, "several clergymen of the city" were requested to attend and officiate at a mass funeral the next day.

With decisions made, committees appointed, and responsibilities delegated, positive results quickly ensued. The city council, for example, approved $300 to aid the victims. Residents subscribed another $500. In year 2000, that $800 amount would have been equivalent to about $17,600.[168]

Burying the Dead

Friday evening, April 9, at the Machpelah Cemetery, a mass burial took place. Workmen dug a long trench in "Potters Field," the section of the cemetery reserved for the indigent. Twenty-one bodies were lowered below the ground and buried in an unmarked grave. Next day, ministers conducted a group funeral.[169]

A discrepancy has existed regarding the location of the burial site. Christ's Church, located at Thirteenth and Franklin Streets, recorded the burial, yet no cemetery existed there. The only cemetery operating in Lexington at the time was the Machpelah Cemetery. A late-nineteenth century local history stated that eighty-three *Saluda* victims were buried there, but the basis for that statement is not known.[170] For the entire year of 1852, the Christ's Church records list thirty-one burials and note that twenty-one were *Saluda* victims.[171]

---

[166] Full minutes of the meeting are published in "The Explosion of the Saluda," *Missouri Republican,* April 17, 1852, a reprint article from the *Lexington Express* Extra of April 13, 1852.

[167] The *Savannah Sentinel,* May 1, 1852, reported that the burial was performed "with indecent haste, and without an inquest, or ditches, dug for that purpose." The account further noted, "The *Western Chronicle* charges the sole responsibility of this scandalous impropriety—to call it by no harsher name—upon a Mr. Silas Silver, who it appears, took it upon himself, contrary to the wishes of the citizens of Lexington, and contrary to the express direction of the committee appointed by them 'to take charge of the dead.'"

[168] *Lexington Express* Extra, April 13, 1852. Clark, "Dollar Calculations Information Sheet," typescript, 5pp., in authors' file, in 1852, the dollar value was about twenty-two times less than it is today.

[169] The burial records for Christ's Church Parish of Lexington for April 9, 1852, states: "buried 21 persons killed by explosion of steamer, *Saluda*: names unknown." See Jacki Gray, "Men Mastered the River Which Molded Their Character," *The Ray County Mirror,* April 1987. The burial took place Friday night and the funeral services on Saturday morning.

[170] *History of Lafayette County, Mo.* (St. Louis: Missouri Historical Company, 1881), 285.

[171] Pete Schaperkotter to Ruth M. White, September 22, 1990, in White's *Saluda* files, Ogden, Utah.

Dr. William M. Bowring's 1852 diary, cited above, says eighty-three were buried in Lexington.[172] His is the only source for that large a number, and newspaper and church sources do not support that claim. Perhaps the doctor heard a casualty figure, heard of the mass burial, and presumed the casualty number was, in fact, a burial number.

Administering Two Estates

Stephen G. Wentworth was Lafayette County's administrator, an elected position.[173] His work included handling estates of deceased people. With the *Saluda* smoke just clearing, he faced dealing with two estate matters involving boat passengers killed in the accident. One was for Jonathan Brock, who was bound for California, and the other was for Duncan Campbell, one of the Mormon emigrants.

Information about Brock comes from an affidavit Jason Abbott filed with Lafayette County justice of the peace, Henry C. Wallace. A supporting affidavit came from Byron B. Lambson. These testimonies say that Abbott met Brock in Springfield, Illinois, where they agreed to travel together to California. For safekeeping purposes, Abbott gave Brock three $10 gold pieces and one 20 frank gold piece [$33.80]. At St. Louis, they boarded the *Saluda* and roomed together on the voyage upriver.

When the *Saluda* blew up, Brock was thrown onto the wharf, where he died, Lampson said. Abbott saw Brock before Brock died. Learning that money found on Brock's body was being held by administrator Wentworth, Abbott went to Mr. Wentworth, told his story, and was allowed to examine the gold pieces among the money. Those coins included the denominations he said he had given to Brock, so he filed a claim for his money from Brock's "estate."

Byron Lampson testified that he became acquainted with victim Brock on the trip up from St. Louis. He frequently saw Brock and Abbott together on the boat. Brock told him that he and Abbott were going to California, whereupon Lampson told them he also was headed to California in the Drake and Sinclair Company and was authorized to engage people to go in that company for a $50 fee and for helping to drive cattle to California. Brock talked about joining the company, saying he had enough money to pay for himself and almost enough of Jason Abbott's money for Abbott to join the company, too.

On Brock's body was found $108.80, a note for $7.50 owed him, and personal property. Three court-appointed citizens appraised the value of personal possessions found on Brock's body; they said $2.25 for a broken silver watch, 75 cents for a dirk knife, $1.75 for a pistol, and 25 cents for his pocket wallet, for total value of $5.00. On April 10, weighing the facts, Wentworth

---

172 Charles Ekin, ed., *Diary of a Town, Wellington, Missouri* (April 9, 1852 diary entry of Dr. William M. Bowring).

173 *History of Lafayette County, Mo.,* 627, states, "In 1851 he [Wentworth] was appointed administrator of public affairs for this county, which office he held until 1864."

awarded Abbott $33.80 (about $740 in year 2000 value). Three years later, the court issued a final settlement of Brock's estate. At that point, after appraisal and court fees were taken out, the estate amounted to $67.95 (about $1,500 in 2000), which belonged, Mr. Wentworth noted, to "kins of said deceased, not known."

Administrator Wentworth's second *Saluda* estate matter involved the money and property belonging to Mormon emigrant Duncan Campbell, killed in the explosion. Court records say that $187.97 cash ($4,135) was found on Campbell's body, along with a badly torn promissory note for $100 ($2,200), signed by Eli Kelsey, and a watch worth $5 ($110). From the cash, the court paid $3 to Silas Silver for burying the corpse, $14.25 to the coroner for inquest costs, $3 to repair Campbell's watch, and various administrative costs, including a final settlement notice posted in the newspaper. When the estate was settled more than a year later (July 1853), the balance, including nearly $20 in interest, stood at $266.32. This estate belonged to Campbell's orphaned son, to be administered by the man whom the court appointed to be the boy's legal guardian, Lexington resident Alexander H. McFadden. (See discussion about the orphans below)

Visits by Mormons

Elder Eli B. Kelsey's little company, which had disembarked at Brunswick to buy cattle, heard about the *Saluda* disaster when they were in Gallatin, Daviess County, sixty miles north of Lexington. In the group were George May and son James, whose family had stayed on the *Saluda*. "As may be supposed there was consternation in our little camp," James May recalled, "and everything bad was thought of." Kelsey, who had several thousand dollars worth of merchandise on the boat, hastened to the scene, arriving in Lexington on Easter Sunday, April 11. He visited the wounded, giving such aid and comfort as he could. Being responsible for the group, even though he had been on land moving some of their cattle toward Council Bluffs, he tried to find out the exact number of the persons killed and wounded. But because so many had left "so quickly and promiscuously" on the *Isabel,* Kelsey could not establish an accurate tally.

When Kelsey returned to the cattle group, George and James May were pleased to learn that "our family was safe" with the exception of one daughter, Harriet, who had an injured foot.[174]

Heavy river traffic in 1852 meant that many travelers passed Lexington, where *Saluda* wreckage was still visible. River talk allowed companies of Mormons to hear about the tragedy when they passed by. In the days immediately following the explosion, a few Mormons, whose boats stopped at Lexington, tried to look in on Mormon victims still in town. One such visitor was John S. Higbee, who had presided over the Mormon company on

---

[174] Reminiscences of James May, 12, LDS Church Archives.

the *Kennebec,* many of whom he had bid farewell to when they boarded the *Saluda.* With him was John Spiers, who recorded their Lexington visit, and a man named Pack and many of the *Kennebec* Mormons who had opted not to go on the *Saluda.* Two weeks after the *Saluda* left St. Louis, this group did, too. Viewing their former shipmates in the aftermath of the explosion was sobering. "Went up the Missouri River to Lexington," Spiers noted. "Several persons who had crossed the ocean with us lay there badly scalded, it was a very depressing sad sight to see them."[175]

The Mystery of the Orphans

That Lexington people adopted Mormon orphans is true, but how many, who they were, and what became of them are questions whose answers are shrouded in mystery. Four stories of orphans have come to light. The fate of one orphan, Duncan Kelsey Campbell, is well documented. Unfortunately, one tradition in Lexington, not seen as untrue, is that a couple named Boulware adopted a Mormon orphan they named Katie Boulware. The third story was unraveled by the relatives of John Sargent, in Utah, who tracked down one of his orphaned sons. A girl named Kramer is a fourth orphan who has been positively identified.

Duncan Kelsey Campbell. As noted in chapter four, Duncan Campbell, his wife, and two children were killed by the explosion. Only son Duncan Kelsey Campbell survived. He was slightly wounded. When Eli Kelsey reached Lexington on Easter Sunday (see above), he intended to return to Lexington at a later date and take the boy to Utah with him and adopt him as his own son. No doubt the boy's middle name of Kelsey was designated because of the Campbell family's high regard for Elder Kelsey. But Kelsey had major responsibilities for the rest of 1852, which included leading a wagon train to Utah, in which many of the *Kennebec* and/or *Saluda* passengers traveled (see chapter six).

On May 11, 1852, Lafayette County Probate Court Judge Edward Stratton ordered that Lexington resident Alexander H. McFadden be appointed guardian of one of the orphans, Duncan Campbell's young namesake son.[176] By an act of the General Assembly of Missouri, in or about 1852, the boy's name was changed legally to George C. McFadden and he was declared to be Alexander McFadden's legal heir.[177]

In July 1855, administrator Wentworth awarded to Mr. McFadden the remaining moneys in deceased Duncan Campbell's estate. From the $319.77 amount, which included interest accrued, costs for a coroner's inquest, taxes, and final settlement notice were taken out, and a $100 promissory note from Eli Kelsey was uncollected. So after Mr. McFadden posted a bond, he received

---

[175] Reminiscences and Journal of John Spiers, 228 (though pages are not numbered), LDS Church Archives.

[176] Lafayette County Probate Records, courthouse annex, Lexington, Missouri.

[177] Statement to Lafayette County Court, subscribed November 10, 1879, Lafayette County Probate Records.

$170 to use for the benefit of the boy. But the Eli Kelsey $100 receipt was left uncollected, so the final estate amounted to $170. Mr. Wentworth determined that because Alexander H. McFadden by then was the legal guardian of Alexander Campbell's young son, McFadden should receive the estate money. He had to post bonds guaranteeing he would use the money for the benefit of the boy.[178]

Apparently, the McFaddens raised adopted son George to adulthood. Alexander McFadden filed a will on October 9, 1882, and died soon after. His will, probated on January 27,1883, made Rachel S. McFadden the executor responsible to pay his "debts, dues, and liabilities." She received the household property, notes, bonds, and debts. To adopted son George C. McFadden (Duncan Campbell's orphan son), about age thirty, he bequeathed but a solitary dollar.[179]

Kate Boulware. Was Kate Boulware one of the orphans from the *Saluda?* Local traditions says so, but census and death records indicate she was not born until a few years after the *Saluda* blew up.

Records show that Dr. William P. and Deborah F. Boulware adopted a girl who was named Mary Boulware and had another girl, whether adopted or not is not clear, named Kate Boulware. In 1852, when the *Saluda* blew up, Mary was age eleven and Kate was not born yet. The 1850 census says the Boulware household consisted of William P. Boulware, age thirty-seven, D. (Deborah) Fleetwood Boulware, age thirty, and Mary A. Bale, a nine-year-old born in England. Ten years later, the census shows that the only child in the home was Mary, age eighteen.

Daughter Mary married William J. Hawkins on October 18, 1866. Justice of the Peace G. Clayton performed the ceremony.[180] Apparently, Mary married again, to a Charles Ketchum. After Mary married and left home, Mrs. Boulware's will specified that trustees sell the Boulware house and lots and from the proceeds pay for her grave and for a headstone for her and her late husband. She requested, too, that $600 go to a trustee in St. Louis to be used for the benefit of her adopted daughter Mary, wife of Charles Ketchum, and her children. Additionally, $100 should go to Mary and $100 to the other daughter, Kate M. Boulware. Kate, too, would receive "all my materials for fancywork."[181]

The 1870 census lists William and Deborah Boulware with four others in the home: a twenty-five-year-old male, a domestic servant named Amelia Estele, who was born in Missouri about 1852; a ten-year-old daughter named Katie McGines, born in Missouri; and eleven-year-old Hattie Hutches. Taking that census enumeration at face value, the Kate M Boulware whom local

---

[178] Copy, Guardian Bond, July 11, 1855, in Lafayette County Probate Records.

[179] Lafayette County Probate Records.

[180] Lafayette County Marriage Records in courthouse annex, Lexington, Missouri.

[181] Lafayette County Probate Records.

traditions says was a *Saluda* orphan was in fact Katie McGines, born about 1860. Likewise, the 1880 census shows only two in the Boulware household: mother Deborah, age fifty, a widow and school teacher, and Kate M. Boulware, described as an "adopted daughter," single, twenty years old, an assistant school teacher, born in New York (not Missouri as listed in the 1870 census).

Lafayette County marriage records show that Kate M. Boulware married Gustav Gruber on April 21 or May 2, 1883 (there is some confusion in the record). The 1900 census shows Katie as part of the Gustav Gruber household. She is listed as age forty-two, born in September 1857, married, and with three children. But the census says the three children were from parents born in Ireland, which means the Grubers had adopted them or were their foster parents: Elizabeth, born June 1874, Casper Gruber, born 1888, and Robert, born 1894.

Kate M. Boulware Gruber died on March 25, 1901. Her headstone says she was forty-two years old and hence was born about 1858. Her husband, Gustav Gruber, wrote a will dated October 14, 1903, in which he bequeathed his estate to a daughter named Bessie (Elizabeth) E. Bulford and to sons Casper William Gruber and Robert Gustav Gruber.

Based on census, court, and death records, then, neither of the Boulwares' daughters could have been *Saluda* orphans.

Mary Kramer (Cramer). Lafayette County probate records show that on May 5, 1855, the court appointed Casper Gruber to be the guardian of the person and estate of a Mary Gramer (should be Cramer instead of Gramer), who was a minor and orphan. To fill that role, he was required to file a $200 bond. Surprisingly, the 1860 census does not list her as part of the Casper Gruber household.

Mary married John Sims. They had five children: Elizabeth, Mollie, Lou (Lulu or Louise), John, and James. Some of Mary and John's grandchildren were still living in Lexington in the early 1980s.[182] When a *Saluda* monument was dedication in 1991 (see chapter six), Mr. and Mrs. Robert Schwab attended. His great-great-grandmother, Mary Kramer, was one of the children adopted. Robert knew nothing of his background until told it by his high-school teacher, Elizabeth Gruber, which his mother then verified. Mary had been pulled from the river after the explosion in 1852. She was too young to remember her name but, as Mr. Schwab was told, she was raised by a Gruber family in Lexington.[183]

The Sargent Children. A Lexington family took in the four surviving Sargent children and offered to pay their way back to England—but only if the children would give up their Mormon faith. The children, however, wanted to go to Utah. One daughter, Ellen, chose to remain in Lexington as an adopted child. Ellen married Louis Bremmer on December 4, 1861, at St.

[182] Berbert, "Disaster on the Missouri," 30.
[183] Ruth M. White to Norma N. King, December 5, 1998, copy in White's *Saluda* files, Ogden, Utah.

Louis. They had a daughter named Lou, who married a Mr. Bodecker. The three other children—Sarah Ann, 16, Louisa, 10, and John Jr., 17—eventually went to Utah. Later, John moved to California. They and Ellen kept in touch by correspondence. Ellen died young, about age twenty-eight, on November 5, 1868.[184]

Others? There is evidence that Mary Kramer had a brother who survived the explosion and ended up being adopted by a St. Louis family. Mary's own efforts to locate him did not succeed.[185] However, neither records nor folklore identify, thus far, any other *Saluda* orphans possibly adopted in Lafayette County or nearby. "Several children" is the general term used to enumerate the orphans.

While credit is due the kind families who adopted Duncan Kelsey Campbell (renamed George McFadden), Mary Kramer, and Ellen Sargent, it could be that others were adopted but that fact was hidden and was never told to the children while they were growing up. Also, as historian Dan Spies noted, some of the orphaned children had relatives who tried to locate and claim them, but "some of the townspeople who took in these children were later reluctant to give them up to relatives or friends."[186]

William Dunbar, who lost his wife and two children in the *Saluda* disaster—his entire family—entertained tiny doubts the rest of his life that the badly battered little girl's body he saw in the Lexington makeshift hospital was his daughter. Years later he wrote:

> I have on several occasions since reasoned on the possibility of my being mistaken in identifying the body as that of my child, and wondered if it could be possible that my little girl was among those who fell into the hands of the special committee appointed by the citizens of Lexington to take care of the orphan children. Some of the people, into whose care those children were entrusted, were very reluctant to give them up when asked to do so by relatives and friends; and it is quite possible that one or two of them were never recovered. Some of the citizens, although extremely kind to the unfortunates, would perhaps be conscientious in believing they were doing a good deed in preventing them from being sent to Utah.[187]

Work Well Done

Saluda survivors who wrote about their experiences, including William Dunbar, paid high praise to the community of Lexington and its

---

[184] Ruth M. White to Norma N. King, December 5, 1998.

[185] "Mary Kramer," Ruth M. White research notes, 5 pp. typescript, in White's *Saluda* files, Ogden, Utah.

[186] Spies Term Paper, 14; Jacki Gray, "Men Mastered the River Which Molded Their Character," *The Ray County Mirror*, April 1987, 4.

[187] Jenson, "Fifty-sixth Company," 412.

good people who showed so much concern, kindness, and charity to the explosion victims.

While in Lexington that Easter Sunday checking on Mormon victims, Eli Kelsey felt very grateful for the generous aid the city and its residents were rendering. So he, Abraham Smoot, William Dunbar, and David J. Ross united in a card of thanks to the citizens for their generous and noble conduct.[188]

Smoot, who spent ten days at Lexington helping to encourage and monitor the health of injured Mormons being cared for there, deeply appreciated what the citizenry did for those who needed the help. His comments serve as a lasting tribute and memorial to Lexington from the Latter-day Saints:

> I shall never forget the kindness of the citizens of Lexington in caring for the living and burying the dead. The Lord certainly inspired them to do all that sympathy and benevolence could suggest in aid of the afflicted. The city council set apart a piece of ground in which to bury the Saints who had died, and William H. Russell, the great government freighter, and many other prominent citizens did all they could to comfort and help the afflicted survivors. Besides their devoted attentions, their contributions in aid of the Saints amounted to thousands of dollars.[189]

---

[188] Jenson, "Fifty-sixth Company," 410.
[189] Jenson, "Fifty-sixth Company," 414.

CHAPTER SIX

Aftermath and
Legacy

The bell that rung for this boat's departure, was a tremendous bell; it
swung to and fro awfully; it was big enough for a Cathedral.[190]

About the same time the mass funeral was taking place in Lexington, the
Missouri River steamer *Clara* docked in St. Louis with a tragic cargo. On
board were the bodies of Captain Francis Belt and Second Clerk Jonathan
Blackburn. A large number of friends, the *Missouri Republican* noted, accompanied the bodies to the residences of relatives.[191] On April 17, 1852, at the
Boatman's Church in St. Louis, the Reverend Charles G. Jones preached
funeral sermons for Captain Belt and Blackburn.[192] Captain Belt was thirty-
six and left behind "a helpless and afflicted wife" and three children.[193] His
grave is marked by an imposing Belt family monument in the Lax Cemetery
just northwest of Jerseyville, Illinois, which is north of St. Louis.[194]

In mid-April, unmarried clerk Jonathan Blackburn's body went to the
Bellefontane Cemetery in St. Louis, then to a family cemetery. He left behind
him "an afflicted family to mourn his death."[195]

Then, on April 16, the steamers *El Paso* and *Timour No. 2* arrived at St.
Louis. Peter Conrad, half-owner of the *Saluda,* was on the *El Paso.* He was
badly scalded, and doubts were entertained about his recovery. He convalesced
at his residence and lived another thirty years to age 81.[196] Mate William
Hemler, uninjured, accompanied Mr. Conrad.[197] When Conrad and Hemler
left Lexington, probably on April 12, the *Saluda,* they said, was sunk to her
lower deck, and her bow was out of the water. They reported that the bodies
of pilots Charles La Barge and pilot Louis Guerette had not yet been
found (they never were found) and that First Clerk Brockman was still in

---

[190] T. B. Thorpe, on the riverboat *Emperor* in 1844, quoted in *Before Mark Twain*, 88.

[191] *Missouri Daily Republican,* April 12, 1852, 2.

[192] *Missouri Daily Republican,* April 17, 1852, 3.

[193] *Missouri Daily Republican,* April 12, 1852, 2.

[194] Paul Hokanson to Fred G. Woods, email, February 21, 2002, copy in authors' file.

[195] *Missouri Daily Republican,* April 12, 1852, 2.

[196] "Death of Capt. Peter Conrad," *Waterways Journal* 13, no. 16 (1900): 7.

[197] "River Intelligence," *Missouri Daily Republican,* April 17, 1852, 2.

Lexington, using "every exertion to secure from the wreck everything uninjured."[198]

For the rest of 1852 and into 1853, the *Saluda*'s visible wreckage proved to be one of those "must-see" sights for travelers passing Lexington on the Missouri River. Latter-day Saint Daniel Tyler wrote the following in his diary on August 19, 1853 – sixteen months after the explosion: "5 pm passed Lexington MO. where lays the ruins of the ever memorable *Saluda* by whose disaster the lives of more than a score of Saints were momentarily taken by bursting her boiler—last year." That view prompted him to write a verse:[199]

O *Saluda*, *Saluda* thou treacherous thing!

Thine acts prove that death is on the wing

But if thou art on conquest bent

Remember thy stealth has only taken what was lent.

Saluda Survivors after Lexington

Despite personal injuries and the loss of loved ones, *Saluda* survivors eventually found ways to reach the destinations they had planned prior to the explosion. Almost all passengers had destinations other than Lexington in mind when they bought their *Saluda* tickets. Cabin passengers, very few Mormons among them, and some deck passengers were heading to towns farther upriver in Missouri to pursue personal or business ventures or to begin treks west among the hordes heading for the gold fields that year. Mormons, most of whom were deck passengers, wanted to reach the Council Bluffs area to join wagon trains preparing to head for Utah.

Cabin passengers listed in the *Saluda*'s registry include these names and their destinations:[200]

G. Bentley	Independence
James Wycuff	Independence
James Shymer	Independence
Mr. Hamilton	Independence
Abraham Fisher	Independence
W. Rose	Independence
G. Dilber	Independence
B. H. Samspon	Independence
Mrs. Sampson	Independence
R. Gunn and lady	Independence
M. Sampson	Independence
Mr. Knapp	Independence
Mr. Foleylluber	Independence
Mr. McCallister	Liberty

---

[198] "River Intelligence," *Missouri [Daily] Republican,* April 17, 1852, 2.

[199] Diary of Daniel Tyler, August 19, 1853, LDS Church Archives.

[200] "The Explosion of the Saluda," *Missouri Republican,* April 17, 1852, article reprinted from the *Lexington Express* Extra, April 13, 1852.

R. Fale	Kansas (City)
F. Sternes	Kansas (City)
J. M. Payne	Kansas (City)
J. Murphy, lady and negro	Weston
Bowles and sister	Weston
W. J. Murphy	Weston
J. Cole	St. Joseph
R. Nash	St. Joseph
Mr. Abbott	St. Joseph
Mr. Letcher	St. Joseph
Mr. Lamb	St. Joseph
Mr. Holmes	St. Joseph
John P. Sutton	Iowa Point
Abner Martin and lady	Council Bluffs
Miss Whitaker	Council Bluffs
Miss Randall	Council Bluffs
Mr. Tillard	Council Bluffs
F. Bayless	Kanesville
J. T. Carter	Kanesville

Heavy Overland Trail Traffic

In the three-decade history of the overland trails, 1852 was by far the busiest emigration year. Gold rush and Mormon traffic that year set records, as the following chart shows:[201]

Overland Emigration to Oregon, California, and Utah

Year	Oregon	California	Utah
1849	450	25,000	1,500
1850	6,000	44,000	2,500
1851	3,600	1,100	1,500
1852	10,000	50,000	10,000
1853	7,500	20,000	8,000
1854	6,000	12,000	3,167

While crossing the plains, wagon trains were rarely out of sight of another wagon company. So many wagons left from the St. Joseph vicinity on the same day in 1852 that they commenced their journey twelve abreast.[202] With the multitudes heading to the West, steamboat traffic up the Missouri River during the weeks after the *Saluda's* demise was extremely heavy, too.

Cholera stalked the river regions that year. A contagious virus, spread by flies and human contact, it claimed numerous victims on the river boats, in

---

[201] Adaptation of chart in John Unruh Jr., *The Plains Across: The Overland Immigrants and the Trans-Mississippi West, 1840–1860* (Urbana and Chicago: University of Illinois Press, 1979), 120.

[202] Unruh, *The Plains Across*, 119.

the outfitting camps, and in the wagon trains. One 1852 company of seventy-two men lost one-third of them to cholera, leaving them barely enough men able to drive the teams.[203]

Late in 1851, the First Presidency of The Church of Jesus Christ of Latter-day Saints instructed that all Mormons in the Midwest close down their temporary farms and homes and go to Utah the next year. As a result, more Mormons were on the overland trails in 1852 than in any other year. Most of the Mormons who survived the *Saluda* tragedy managed to trickle into Council Bluffs individually. There, they joined one of twenty-three Mormon-organized wagon companies.[204] Eli Kelsey, initially a leader on the *Saluda,* captained one of those wagon trains, with several *Saluda* survivors.

Among the dozens of *Saluda* survivors in those companies, some fell victim to the cholera plague. In 1852, no less than ninety-nine people died of cholera in the Mormon wagon trains or encampments.[205]

Abraham O. Smoot, after tending to *Saluda* victims for ten days and buying livestock for the wagon companies, returned to St. Louis. From there he went upriver to Atchison, Kansas Territory. There, he became captain of a wagon train. Before the group could depart, cholera infested their camp, too. "There were over forty cases, and of these some fifteen proved fatal," he reported. Others "were healed instantaneously through the prayer of faith when the Elders laid their hands upon them." During the first part of the journey, Smoot himself caught the cholera, which prostrated him. Through the faith and prayers of his company, he said, he recovered, albeit seventy-five pounds lighter.[206]

Other travelers proved not so fortunate in escaping the death-grip of cholera. By mid-June, the May family, which had seven members on the *Saluda* and two going overland, reunited safely and joyfully at Council Bluffs about the middle of June. But their jubilee was short-lived. Before they could head out for Utah, cholera struck the family, killing the father, George, and the eldest and youngest daughters. Then, when the rest started for the Missouri River ferry, one of the sons died. Soon, the mother died, too. "Now there were 4 of us orphan children," young James May said later, who all went west in Eli Kelsey's wagon company.[207]

Henry Ballard, the May family's friend, who helped those who were on the *Saluda,* traveled west with the Mays. "I also took the same disease but

---

[203] Unruh, *The Plains Across,* 124.

[204] Stanley B. Kimball, *Historic Resource Study: Mormon Pioneer National Historic Trail* (Washington, D.C.: United States Department of Interior/National Park Service, 1991),139–41.

[205] Melvin L. Bashore to the authors, email, February 21, 2002, copy in authors' files. Mr. Bashore is a reference librarian at the LDS Church Historical Department in Salt Lake City, Utah. See also Roger P. Blair, "'The Doctor Gets some Practice': Cholera and Medicine on the Overland Trails," *Journal of the West* 34 (January 1997): 54–66.

[206] Smoot, in *Early Scenes in Church History,* 28, Jenson, Church Chronology, 46 notes that Smoot's company was met by the First Presidency, Wm. Pitt's Brass Band and leading citizens at Emigration Canyon.

[207] James May Reminiscences, 9-13.

---

through the blessings of the Lord it passed off with no very bad effect upon me," he said. The Kelsey Company reached Utah in mid-October. Ballard served as an LDS bishop in Logan, Utah, from 1861 to 1900. His son, Melvin J. Ballard, became an LDS Church apostle, as did his great-grandson M. Russell Ballard.[208]

The Harry Brown family survived the explosion, except for the severely injured father, who died three weeks later. The others reached Council Bluffs and set out for Utah on July 14. Son Ira's leg, badly broken in the explosion, became infected, forcing the family to stop at Fort Laramie, where his leg was amputated. Daughter Sarah continued on to Utah in the Henry Miller Company, while the family waited a year for Ira to heal. Sarah married LDS Church Apostle Wilford Woodruff in 1853. She was the mother of eight children. He became the Church's president in 1889.[209]

Agnes Cook Gillespie, who stayed in Lexington "a long time" to recover from being scalded, went with husband Alexander to Council Bluffs, joined the Kelsey Company, and went to Utah.[210]

Adolphia and Rhoda Byrne Young and their family stayed in Lexington for six weeks while their damaged belongings were repaired. After Adolphia bought oxen, cows, a wagon, and tent, the family traveled from Lexington in comparative comfort to Council Bluffs. They joined Captain John Tidwell's company. Heading west, Adolphia died on July 5, and oldest son Sammie died three days later. The rest of the family arrived in Utah in mid-September.[211]

And what of William C. Dunbar, the man with three expired chances not to be on the *Saluda* and ended up losing his wife and two children when it exploded? He reached Utah that year, fulfilled a proselytizing mission in England and France, and remarried in Utah. He was a famous comedian, vocalist, and bagpipe performer in the early days of Salt Lake City. Later, he helped found the *Salt Lake Herald* newspaper. In later years, his faith cooled. He died in Salt Lake City in 1905.[212]

The annual Mormon emigrations with long trips up the Mississippi ended in 1855 when church leaders decided travel would be safer and less expensive by railroad travel from East Coast ports to Iowa City or to Quincy, Illinois.[213] After this time, voyages up the "Big Muddy," were limited to those Mormon migrants who journeyed from St. Louis to the West.

---

[208] Henry Ballard Reminiscences and Diary 1–4; "Henry Ballard," *LDS Biographical Encyclopedia*, 1:419.

[209] *Our Pioneer Heritage*, 10:235–36; John L. Hart, "Restored Cabin a Remnant of Faith," *Church News*, May 29, 1993, 6.

[210] *Our Pioneer Heritage*, 19:416–17.

[211] *Our Pioneer Heritage*, 6:184–85.

[212] *LDS Biographical Encyclopedia*, 4:335.

[213] This change was stimulated by a letter dated August 2, 1854, in which Brigham Young instructed Elder Franklin D. Richards, a Latter-day Saint emigration agent at Liverpool, to no longer use New Orleans because of the threat of river disease. See "Foreign Correspondence," *Millennial Star* 16 (October 28, 1854): 684.

Steamboat Safety Reforms

During the winter months before the *Saluda* tragedy, the United States Congress had been considering stricter steamboat laws. The Senate approved a bill called "An Act to Provide for the Better Security of Passengers On Board of Vessels Propelled in Whole or in Part by Steam." One reform bill died in the House in February, whereupon a new bill was introduced. But then came the *Saluda* explosion and three more disasters within a four-week period. The other three and their locations, dates, and casualties were as follows:

Pocahontas	lower Mississippi	March 14, 1852	8 scalded to death
Red Stone	Ohio	April 2, 1852	20 killed
Glencoe	St. Louis levee	April 3, 1852	60 killed

Two months after the *Saluda* explosion, Senator John Davis of Massachusetts, chairman of the Commerce Committee, called representatives of southern and western steamboat owners and masters to a convention at Louisville to discuss proposed new regulations. Steamboatmen at this meeting urged more safeguards for boilers, "but high pressure boat operators in the West opposed regulatory limits on maximum allowable steam pressure for vessels then in use. They urged more competent examinations for engineers and pilots, examinations for masters and mates, and river traffic regulations for avoiding collisions." During Senate consideration of new legislation, the Davis Bill, Alfred Guthrie prepared a comprehensive report about the causes of steamboat boiler explosions, based on an examination of eight hundred boats on western waters in eight months. The Senate passed a new regulation bill and sent it to the House.[214]

Shortly after the House received the Davis bill, the steamer *Henry Clay* burned, on the Hudson River, which helped inspire the House to pass the Davis Bill on August 25. Now, new and stricter regulations were on the books, with enforcement provisions dealing with maximum allowable steam pressures, operating rules, examinations for officers, and a system of inspectors. But, although the law was on the books, little was done to enforce it until 1871.[215]

End of the Steamboat Era

In 1869, the transcontinental railroad made crossing the continent faster, easier, and less expensive. As connecting lines were built and as more and more communities obtained railroad service, the era of steamboats hauling passengers and freight gradually declined. But the tradition was too strong to die completely. Ever more palatial river boats were built to serve the leisure class as hotels and casinos.[216]

---

[214] Spies, Saluda Paper, 19-23. Spies cites Miscellaneous Documents of the Senate, No. 32, 32nd Cong., 1st S.

[215] Spies, Saluda Paper, 24; Ron Larson, *Upper Mississippi River History: Fact-Fiction- Legend* (Winona, Minnesota: Steamboat Press, 1994):12.

[216] Hunter, *Steamboats on the Western Rivers*, 585–640 explains how transportation via railroads triumphed over steamboats and the needed adjustments the steamboat industry made to continue business on a more moderate scale.

The *Saluda's* Bell and Other Relics

Records don't say when the last bits of the *Saluda's* wreckage finally disappeared from the Lexington waterfront. The *Saluda's* bell, blown some seventy yards up the river bank, survived in good shape. Made of metal more than two inches thick, the bell is more than three feet in diameter, has a heavy clapper cast in one piece, and features an engraved "Diana" on its side. Since then, the story of the *Saluda* has generated a curious drama involving Lexington and the city of Savannah, Missouri. A local junk dealer picked up the forsaken bell for salvage.[217] A month or so later, Elder Prince L. Hudgens of the Savannah Christian Church came to town. He needed a bell for his new church, saw the *Saluda's* bell was for sale, and bought it for $17.50. The *Savannah Sentinel,* in its May 22, 1852, issue, reported on his purchase:

> Bell Arrival—the handsome bell, which was attached to the ill-fated "Saluda" which blew up at Lexington some time since, is now in the belfry of the Christian church of this place. We should judge from its full-toned vibrations, which almost daily strike our ears, that it received no damages from the awful explosion, which launched so many souls into eternity. We hope its career may prove more peaceful—from being the herald of a "sea monster" to a Christian's chime awakening church going memories![218]

Back in 1847, the Church of the Disciples was organized in Savannah, a town sitting beside the Missouri River just north of St. Joseph. Members built a brick church there in 1851, on the corner of Fifth and Market Streets. Elder Prince L. Hudgens became the church's pastor in 1852, and that's when he bought the *Saluda* bell. He continued in his ministry until the Civil War broke out in 1861. The original church was replaced in 1894, and the bell was transferred to the new church. When that church was replaced in 1959, the congregation created a decorative memorial wall in front of it with a nook in which the *Saluda* bell now hangs, "having rung out its invitation to come and worship" for 150 years.[219]

In 1935, the Lexington Commercial Club talked of building a memorial park and tower to honor the *Saluda* and its victims. A committee went to Savannah to buy the *Saluda* bell for the proposed tower. But older members of the Savannah church protested, so the bell stayed where it was.[220] Subsequent attempts by the people of Lexington to obtain the bell have likewise failed.

Other parts of the *Saluda* survive. Its dinner bell and a small pulley now are housed in the Battle of Lexington State Historic Site. The Lexington Historical Museum has two large wooden pulleys, weighing a hundred

---

[217] Spies, Saluda Paper, 7.

[218] *Savannah Sentinel,* May 22, 1852.

[219] Williams, *History of Northwest Missouri,* 316; *Andrew County A Community* (Andrew County Historical Society, 1980), 203.

[220] *Kansas City Journal-Post,* March 27, 1938.

pounds each, and a large whetstone, its wooden case having burn marks on it. Several doors from the *Saluda* have been used in local homes. One of those was hanging for years in the Marie Gruber Stiles home. After Marie's death, it was recovered from her home, which had been destroyed by fire. After the door was stripped of many coats of white paint, it was hung in Lexington's Log House Museum, an 1830s log cabin. This cabin once stood on Highland Avenue, overlooking the dock site where the *Saluda* disaster happened.[221]

The *Saluda*'s pilot wheel survived, but its whereabouts is unknown. In 1933, it was at the Wentworth Military Academy in Lexington and had been turned into a coat rack.[222]

Machpelah Cemetery Monument

On September 19, 1991, descendants of John Sargent, who was killed in the *Saluda* accident, dedicated a monument in Lexington's Machpelah Cemetery to honor all who died on the *Saluda*. Blair P. Pack, a third-great-grandson of John Sargent, dedicated the monument. The text on the monument's plaque reads:[223]

SALUDA MEMORIAL
IN MEMORY OF THOSE WHO LOST THEIR LIVES IN THE EXPLOSION OF THE STEAMBOAT "SALUDA" HERE ON APRIL 9, 1852, MANY OF WHOM ARE BURIED HERE IN A COMMON GRAVE.

THE TOTAL LOSS OF LIFE WAS NEVER DEFINITELY DETERMINED BUT WAS ESTIMATED AT ABOUT ONE HUNDRED, AS MANY WERE BLOWN INTO THE RIVER AND LOST.

MOST OF THE CASUALTIES WERE MORMON CONVERTS EN ROUTE TO SALT LAKE CITY FROM GREAT BRITAIN.

ERECTED 1991
BY JOHN SARGENT DESCENDANTS

The plaque contains the names of the known dead and missing, based on research conducted up to 1991. Funds for the monument were contributed by descendants of two of the Sargent sisters orphaned by the explosion—Sarah Ann and Louisa.[224]

---

[221] "Saluda Door," one-page summary, photocopy, Lexington/Lafayette County Historical Society Museum.

[222] Photocopy, with note, of photograph of the *Saluda* pilot's wheel, Ruth Ferris Collection, Mercantile Library.

[223] "A Saluda Memorial Service," four-page printed program, copy in Ruth M. White's *Saluda* files, Ogden, Utah.

[224] Ruth M. White to *Ensign,* January 23, 1992, copy in Ruth M. White's *Saluda* files, Ogden, Utah.

Epilogue

Good judgment is hard to assess. Did David Ross and Eli Kelsey use bad judgment when they booked the large Mormon company of ninety or more souls on the aging *Saluda?* Poor William Dunbar. Of all the unfortunate passengers, he was the most unlucky one. After feeling prompted not to go on the *Saluda,* he had three clear opportunities not to board the ill-fated boat. Premonitions are hard to judge, too. Because the *Saluda* disaster was the only steamboat catastrophe Mormons experienced in their twenty-eight years of transporting thousands of their people on America's rivers, the leaders who chose that boat have been subjected to criticism.

In the spring of 1850, Mormon Apostle Wilford Woodruff led a group of Mormon emigrants to Utah. In 1898, as President of The Church of Jesus Christ of Latter-day Saints, he related how he felt prompted in 1850 not to go aboard a steamer:[225]

> After spending two years and a half in New England and Canada, getting the Saints out, I started back with the last lot, about a hundred from Boston. We landed in Pittsburgh at dusk. We were anxious not to stay there, but to go on to St. Louis. I saw a steamer making steam ready to go out. I went to the captain and asked him how many passengers he had. "Three hundred and fifty." "Could you take another hundred?" "Yes." I was just about to tell him we wanted to go aboard when that Spirit said to me, "Don't go aboard that steamer, you nor your company." All right said I. I had learned something of that still, small voice. I did not go aboard that steamer, but waited till the next morning. In thirty minutes after that steamer left, it took fire. It had ropes instead of wheel chains, and they could not go ashore. It was a dark night, and not a soul was saved.

Woodruff, who married *Saluda* survivor Sarah Brown in 1853, mentioned the *Saluda* in one of his most reflective diary entries:[226]

> In all the travels & Emigrations of the Saints for the last 40 years the preserving Care of our Heavenly Father has been over us & we as a people have been spared. . . . The destruction of the Saluda is the only Case where the saints have met with disaster

---

[225] President Wilford Woodruff, April conference report, 1898, 30. See also Wilford Woodruff Journals, 3:544–47 for the dates of April 9, 1850, to May 1, 1850.
[226] Wilford Woodruff Journals, 7:57.

in their Emigration, and if Eli B Kelsey who was the leader of the Company had had the spirit of God & his office upon him he never would have gone on board of that Boat or taken the Saints on board of it.

Whether Woodruff was right or wrong, it is clear how fortunate it was that the *Saluda* blew up when it was at Lexington, Missouri, and not out on the river somewhere. Luckily, when disaster struck, the steamboat was close by a community of good people who were able to rescue, nurse, comfort, care for, and assist the victims. In that sense, it was indeed a Good Friday for many of the victims. It was good because it happened at Lexington.

The story of the *Saluda* is a story of tragedy and triumph. It is both dreadful and inspiring. It breathes a spirit of death and horror but also of life and love. To members of The Church of Jesus Christ of Latter-day Saints, it serves as a reminder that although there was a cruel forced exile of Mormons from Missouri, there were also compassionate hearts among Missourians with charity toward the Mormons. Abraham O. Smoot, who was an eyewitness to the catastrophe and the compassion stated, "I shall never forget the kindness of the citizens in caring for the living and burying the dead. The Lord certainly inspired them to do all that sympathy and benevolence could suggest in aid of the afflicted."

In this sesquicentennial year, it is altogether fitting that people should remember not only those who died at Lexington but also the citizenry who breathed a spirit of life, love, and service on victims in need. Visitors find in Lexington today a legacy of that same caring and kindness that existed 150 years ago. This is evidenced by the fact that this year (2002) the city has provided a commemoration honoring those who perished in the *Saluda* explosion as well as a new memorial that contains the names of all the victims. This book, in a small way, is an expression of gratitude and a means of honoring Lexington's goodness.

Beneath Lexington's brow, the muddy Missouri still flows.
At Savannah the strong *Saluda* bell still tolls
Machpelah Cemetery is quiet and green
And the *Saluda* continues to haunt and intrigue.

A Discussion of How Many Died as a Result of the *Saluda* Explosion

A. The Numbers Problem

A mishmash of literature about the *Saluda* disaster—newspaper accounts, county and local histories, maritime journals, and published articles—presents readers with a disconcerting array of numbers regarding how many victims died or were lost. Depending on what source is consulted, estimates range from 26 to 400. Further muddying the numbers water, we find two totals circulating for how many victims were buried in Lexington.

Some totals were produced by subtracting. That is, someone assessed about how many people were on board and then subtracted how many were accounted for, and the balance was those assumed dead or missing. (The assumption that most of the missing were casualties is flawed because many passengers left on their own without notifying anybody and because we lack reports from down river of any bodies washing ashore.) By contrast, other totals were based on actual counts of dead bodies and on reports by survivors about people who were known to be missing. These totals seem the most responsible, but they clearly are also incomplete.

Since the day of the disaster, every report or history concerning the *Saluda* has determined that the total number killed or missing was not obtainable. No accurate count or even reliable approximation seems likely, for four reasons.

First, while a passenger list for the cabin passengers survived, no such list was found for the much more numerous deck passengers.

Second, aside from the known victims whose bodies were retrieved and buried, it is anyone's guess how many dead were blown into the swift river and churned to the bottom of the Missouri River.

Third, at Lexington in days prior to the explosion, an unknown number of *Saluda* passengers left the nonprogressing boat and found substitute transportation to their nearby homes upriver (Weston, Kansas City, Independence, etc.)

Fourth, within three hours of the explosion, the steamboat *Isabel* left Lexington carrying an undetermined number of *Saluda* survivors, gratefully accepting the *Isabel* captain's generous offer of free passage.

In short, we begin with an unknown number of passengers, having no way to estimate how many victims disappeared in the river or how many quietly resumed their journey on their own resources without reporting to authorities. Because we lack this information, a responsible guess of the total number of people killed in this disaster is elusive.

B. Two Generally Accepted Rules for Assessing the Reliability of Evidence

The historian's two general rules of thumb regarding the reliability of information are the following:

1. Information closest to the event tends to be more accurate than that remembered long after.

2. Firsthand information tends to be more reliable than someone reporting what was heard second hand.

C. Assessing the Contemporary Accounts

Account: April 10, 1852, *Missouri Republican*: Third report from Lexington, this one by Captain C. F. Brockman, the *Saluda*'s first clerk, and, hence, one who knew about passenger numbers:

> 30 to 100 killed.
> Seventy Mormons boarded at St. Louis, 8 to 10 of whom disembarked at Brunswick or Boonville.

Account: "Sion!!" *The Daily Missouri Republican* April 10, 1852, 2:

> First dispatch: April 9, Lexington, Saluda exploded with one hundred passengers on board, many of whom were killed.

> Second dispatch: All officers killed and missing except first mate and clerk.

> Third dispatch: from Capt. C. F. Brockman, the first Clerk: Left St. Louis with large crowd of cabin passengers, principal portion of deck passengers were Mormons, seventy of whom boarded her here. Forty-five of these were from the ship *Kennebec*. Remaining 25 were Mississippi families primarily. The whole number of Saints must have been reduced to about sixty, when the explosion took place, as some eight or ten, headed by a Mr. Kelsey, had made preparations previous to leaving this point, to disembark at Brunswick or Boonville, for the purpose of purchasing cattle. Accounts of number killed or lost "vary from 30 to 100."

Account: April 11, 1852 telegraph report. "By Morse's Western Line," *The Missouri Republican,* St. Louis, n.d.:

> List by identification 22 "dead and buried" and 10 as missing.
> Says total thus far: 33 dead or missing.
> Also 10 wounded, 2 mortally.

Account: *Lexington Express,* Extra, of April 13:

26 mangled corpses collected together. "The probability is that the number of killed and badly wounded is about one hundred."

Account: April 14, *St. Joseph Gazette:*

Claims *Saluda* left with 400 passengers, but many cabin passengers disembarked at Lexington before the explosion.

Says firsthand report (reprints article from a newspaper called the *Journal*) claiming 135 lives lost, based on first clerk saying 175 were aboard and only about 50 "are known living," hence a loss of life was not less than 135.

Account: April 16, 1852, *Statesman:*

Cites Mr. Brockman, the first clerk, saying he thought between 80 and100 were killed and missing. But explains, too, that those ashore set number at 126–30. To date, 24 bodies had been recovered.

Account: April 18, 1852, public church meeting in Kanesville/Council Bluffs (account published in *Frontier Guardian and Iowa Sentinel* of April 22, 1852):

Discussed disaster "by which some 20 or 30 [Mormons] were killed, and perhaps an equal number or more of other people shared a similar fate."

Notes that the steamboat *Isabel* "brought several survivors to this place."

Account: Eyewitness Abraham O. Smoot, later published in *The Contributor* 13 (July 1892): 414, who was on the steamboat *Isabel* that lay nearby:

"I went on board of her to visit the Saints (who were in charge of D. J. Ross, Eli B. Kelsey having gone ashore to purchase cattle), and left just before the last plank was drawn in, preparatory to attempting to start. I had not walked to exceed two hundred yards after leaving the Saluda before the explosion occurred, and on turning to look in the direction of the ill-fated boat I saw the bodies of many of the unfortunate passengers and various parts of the boat flying in the air in every direction. Fortunately for the Saints on board, they were mostly on the deck of the boat and pretty well towards the stern, and they consequently fared better than those who were below, or on the forepart of the boat, which was blown entirely to pieces. As it was, however, upwards of twenty of the Saints were lost or subsequently died of their wounds."

Account: Eyewitness Abraham O. Smoot, letter from Lexington to President Brigham Young, Brigham Young Collection, LDS Church Archives:

"On Friday Morning the 7th Inst about 7 Oct The Steamer Saluda on her way from St. Lewis to Council Bluffs (Cargo Principly for that Place) having on bord Old & Young of Our People about 115 Soles made an attempt to Leave this warf with a tremendious waight of steam Her floor is surposed Carlapsed & about the second revolution she Exploded & Litterly blew her all to Peacies . . .

"The nearest Estimate that Can be made of the intire Loss of Life is about 75 Soules out of 175 Passengers the Capt & Pretty much all the Crew was Lost & her intire Cargo of fraight." Note: An edited version of this letter was later published in the *Deseret News,* May 29, 1852, 3.

D. Later Histories (listed in chronological order)

History of Lafayette County, Mo., Carefully Written and Compiled from the Most Authentic Official and Private Sources, Including a History of its Townships, Cities, Towns and Villages (St. Louis: Missouri Historical Company, 1881):

[Has date wrong: says 1851; says explosion at 9 A.M.], 284–85. "**Eighty-three persons were buried at Lexington** from this wreck, and it was never known how many more bodies were lost in the river," 285.

E. W. Gould, *Fifty Years on the Mississippi, or, Gould's History of River Navigation* (St. Louis: Nixon-Jones Printing Co., 1889):

Page 437: *Saluda*: 27 lives lost.

But then contradicts the chart: pp. 478–79, "Explosion of the Saluda": Several of her passengers, because of the delay at Lexington, left her to seek other conveyances. Page 478 says explosion at 1 A.M. "The books were lost, and the names of all the passengers who were killed by the explosion or who sunk with the boat could not be ascertained. The number of those who perished is estimated at one hundred," 478.

William Young, *Young's History of Lafayette County, Missouri* (Indianapolis: B. F. Bowen & Company, 1910):

Account later by eyewitness Col. James Hale.

"On the day after the explosion all the then dead, numbering about thirty, were buried in a long trench in that part of Macpelah cemetery known as Potter's field. Others were buried there who died later or were found. Including the crew, there must have been on the boat at the time of the explosion nearly three hundred people, two hundred of whom were never accounted for."

W. J. MacDonald, "The Missouri River and Its Victims," *The Missouri Historical Review* 21 (July 1927): 581-607:

Saluda. "Captain Belt, Captain Chas LaBarge, pilot, Captain Louis Guerette, second pilot, and about twenty-four others were killed, and a large number wounded [thus, estimates 27], 593.

Dan H. Spies, "The Story of the 'Saluda,'" University of Missouri, an "Arts and Science Dean's Paper," 30 pp., written prior to 1965:

The actual number of persons who lost their lives in the explosion of the "Saluda" will probably never be known. The only official record extant of the burial of the "Saluda" dead in Lexington is an old burial record of Christ Church parish which contains the following entry:

Good Friday, April 9, 1852. Buried 21 persons killed by explosion of steamer Saluda—names unknown.

Burial of these 21 persons was in the old City Cemetery on which now stands a public school building. (Cites interview with late B. M. Little Sr.., Lexington). In addition to these 21 dead the bodies of Capt.

Belt and his first clerk, Mr. Brockman, were taken by steamer to St. Louis for burial. Other accounts of the disaster mention 26 corpses lined up on the river bank. With one exception all of the mentions of the "Saluda" dead buried in Lexington does not exceed 30 individuals. The one exception is an 1881 *History of Lafayette County* which says 83 persons were buried in Lexington from the wreck. Government records of steamboat disasters on the Missouri river, compiled by Capt. Joseph LaBarge, list only 27 killed in the "Saluda" explosion.

Spies favors figure that says 175 person were on board, and only about fifty are known to be living, so "135 to 145 were either killed or missing."

"Residents Research Explosion of Saluda," *The Ogden Utah Examiner,* June 9, 1992:

Quotes Ruth White of Ogden, claiming she is descendant of one of the 40 Mormon survivors. She says of the estimated 175 to 300 passengers, **at least 80 were buried in a common grave at Machpelah cemetery**, and others were lost in the river.

E. Later Accounts in Mormon Histories

Andrew Jenson, "Church Emigration," 1890–93, *Contributor* 12 (July 1892): 408–14:

Some of the *Kennebec* Saints remained temporarily in St. Louis, but a number of those who continued the journey to the Valley that season only tarried in that city a few days; as they took passage on an old dilapidated steamboat, the *Saluda,* which had been chartered by Elders Eli B. Kelsey and David J. Ross, to take a company of Saints up the river to Council Bluffs. On the thirtieth of March she sailed from St. Louis, with about one hundred and seventy-five persons on board, of whom about ninety were Saints.

Cites *Lexington Express Extra,* which says "The probability is that the number of killed and badly wounded is about one hundred." . . .

The passengers and crew of the *Isabel* were eye-witnesses of the explosion, and saw the bodies, and pieces of the doomed boat flying through the air; they made heroic efforts to recover the bodies of those who were killed, as they floated past, but only a few of them were seen and secured. Immediately after the accident, Captain Miller of the *Isabel,* generously offered a free passage to the Bluffs, with provisions, to all who wished to go. Many accepted of the noble offer, and in three hours after the explosion had taken place, they were on their way up the river; the remainder, including the wounded and their immediate relatives and friends, remained behind. . . .

Elder Kelsey, who heard of the explosion while doing business at Gallatin, Daviess County, Missouri, sixty miles north of Lexington, hastened to the scene of the disaster, where he arrived on Sunday, April the eleventh. He immediately visited the wounded, and gave them such aid and comfort as was within his power. Elder A. O. Smoot was with them already, having come up on the steamer *Isabel*, and witnessed the explosion. Elder Kelsey endeavored to find out the exact number of persons killed and wounded, but in consequence of so many leaving so quickly and promiscuously on the *Isabel*, the true number and names of all the killed could not be ascertained, nor has such information been obtained since, so far as the writer of this article has been able to learn. Elder Kelsey reported the following names of Saints killed: (lists 20 and says "and perhaps four or five others. (Note: of the 20 Kelsey identified, little boy Newbury Sargent was never found, nor were two Whitehead children, and some of the 4 missing in the Duncan Campbell family.) He names 5 who were seriously injured. Jenson then named the *Express's* list of 10 not listed by Kelsey who were killed or wounded, and repeated the *Express's* list of 7 missing and 15 that newspaper identified as wounded.

B. H. Roberts, *Comprehensive History of The Church of Jesus Christ of Latter-day Saints.* (1930), 4:78:

The exact number of the killed and wounded is not definitely known, but is given by the Lexington Express, extra, of April 13th, as "about one hundred." Only twenty-six bodies of the killed were recovered.

Geri Berbert, "Disaster on the Missouri," *Ensign,* September 1981, 25–27. (Okay research in Missouri sources but did no research in LDS sources):

Goes with the 83 buried at Lexington and at least that number washed away. Estimates of number of LDS among the dead range as high as 200. "Among the dead were as many as 200 Latter-day Saints en route to the West."

F. Conflicting Reports of Number Buried in Lexington

Supporting the newspaper numbers above:

Eye-witness James Hale later recalled that "On the day after the explosion all the then dead, numbering about thirty, were buried in a long trench in that part of Macpelah cemetery known as Potter's field. Others were buried there who died later or were found." (William Young, *Young's History of Lafayette County, Missouri* (Indianapolis: B. F. Bowen & Company, 1910).

Dan Spies' pre-1865 research paper:

The only official record extant of the burial of the "Saluda" dead in Lexington is an old burial record of Christ Church parish which contains the following entry: "Good Friday, April 9, 1852. Buried 21 persons killed by explosion of steamer Saluda—names unknown."

Spies argues that the burial of these 21 persons was in the old City Cemetery on which now stands a public school building. (Cites interview with late B. M. Little Sr., Lexington). In addition to these 21 dead the bodies of Capt. Belt and his first clerk, Mr. Brockman, were taken by steamer to St. Louis for burial. Other accounts of the disaster mention 26 corpses lined up on the river bank.

Sources for the much-larger figure of 83 burials:

Spies observes that with one exception all of the mentions of the "Saluda" dead buried in Lexington does not exceed 30 individuals. The one exception is an 1881 *History of Lafayette County*, which says 83 persons were buried in Lexington from the wreck.

A *History of Lafayette County, Missouri* . . . (St. Louis: Missouri Historical Company, 1881):285, which gives 1851 date instead of 1852 and has explosion at 9 a.m. instead of earlier, says: "**Eighty-three persons were buried at Lexington** from this wreck, and it was never known how many more bodies were lost in the river."

Dr. William Moore Bowring kept scraps of history, from his easy days as physician in Wellington. Charles Moore Bowring compiled the scraps into the former of a diary in about 1898. C. M. Bowring died January 1926. John Corse then became keeper of the diary. Diary lay in vault in Wellington Bank for years, and was a reference source for dating Wellington happenings. In 1956 Mr John Corse loaned the manuscript to the Missouri State historical Society, who made a typewritten copy. Mr. Corse died in 1966, whereupon wife Wahneta took care of diary until she donated original to Society Library in Columbia. In 1984 Joanne Chiles Eakin reproduced the diary making it available to the public. Citation for it: Joanne Chiles Eakin, *Diary of a Town: Wellington, Missouri* (Independence, Missouri: The Compiler, 1984).

Diary entry: 4/9/1852: Dr. Wm. M. Bowring & Wm. Gordon were sent for to go to Lexington and assist in caring for those injured in the explosion of the steamboat, Saluda at 7 A.M. of that day. "**The number of those receiving burial by citizens was eighty three, but the total loss of life has never been definitely ascertained.**" We ask the question, was this sentence in the original diary or added by the diary compiler? Either this is a statement made at the time, in 1852, and is source for the 1881 history's statement about 83 burials, OR, the diary compiler in the 1890s pulled the 83 number from the 1881 Lafayette County history. Which is it? We bet on the latter. But, even if the former and the entry was made in April 1852, it is still a statement by an outsider that is not corroborated by Lexington church records or the one eye-witness account of the burials, above.

G. Conclusions

Our judgment might not have more merit than any else's, but here is how we are handling the above evidence:

1. The number of eighty-three buried in Lexington is unsubstantiated. The 1881 county history, written three decades later, uses it but gives no

citation. The doctor's compiled diary that used the figure either used a figure the doctor, an outsider at Lexington, heard, or the 1890s compiler of that diary, from the doctor's "scraps," inserted that figure after seeing it in the 1881 history. Contemporary accounts, be it the church's record cited by Mr. Spies or the newspaper accounts, go with the near two dozen figure, and so do we.

2. We feel the Smoot figures are close to correct because (a) he was an eyewitness and (b) he stayed in Lexington to help Mormon victims. He says 175 were on board, using a figure that the *Saluda* clerk also used, and says about two dozen Mormons were killed or definitely missing, and about that same number and maybe a few more non-Mormons were other victims.

3. Eyewitnesses say "several" bodies were blown into the river, not huge numbers. We have no reports that many, or even any, bodies were found down river, so we do not think many were lost to the river. Is it possible that forty or fifty or more bodies went into the river and all went to the bottom? Seems unlikely.

4. It is clear that many cabin passengers left the *Saluda* while it was at Lexington and found their own transportation to their destinations in nearby towns and that "several" survivors left Lexington immediately after the explosion, on board the *Isabel*. Thus, the only "missing" figures that seem responsible are those from family members or close associates who said they knew of someone missing. But even then, it could be that some of these "missing" ones were on the *Isabel* or left Lexington using some other conveyance. Between twelve and fifteen were verified as missing and presumed dead, so there were no doubt others who suffered that same fate but lacked surviving associates at Lexington who could know they were missing.

Finally, here's what we are comfortable with: It seems that between twenty-six and one hundred were killed or lost to the river. Smoot's figures are about right when he says that 175 were on board and about 75 were killed and lost and presumed dead. That's where we are—after reviewing the "facts."

However, if anyone wants to be broader or be safer, we can justifiably say that the mix of records and accounts about the *Saluda* disaster gives widely varying estimates ranging from 26 to 135. Any figures higher than those seem irresponsible. "Close to 100" would be the safer statement to circulate.

The Saluda Passenger/Officer/Crew List

Name	Title	Origin	LDS	Died*	Wounded	Not Wounded	Notes
Abbott, Mr.					y		Slightly injured
Ambuston, Michael				y			
Bailey, Lois Locke		Cambridge, England	y	y			34 years old
Bailey, Mary Ann		Cambridge, England	y	y			31 years old
Ballard, Henry		Scotland	y		y		
Bayless, F.	Captain/Part Owner						
Belt, Francis T.				y			"Francis' father was Henry M. Belt, and his brother was Lloyd T. Belt; Francis had a wife and three children, when he died in his 36th year. He is buried in Green [Jersey] County, IL."
Bentley, G.							
Blackburn, Jonathan	Second Clerk			y			Blackburn is buried in St. Louis; he was found dead near Captain Belt's body.
Bowles, Miss							
Bowles, Mr.							
Brick, J.				y			
Bridges, William H.		New York		y			Yankee Comedian from the McFarland Troop; $108.80 in gold, a pistol, a dirk, and a silver watch were all found on him after the explosion
Brock, Jonathan		Macoupin, IL		y			He later died on April 20 from brain fever.
Brockman, F.C.	First Clerk				y		
Brown, Edward			y		y		2 1/2-year-old son of Harry and Rhoda Brown
Brown, Harry			y		y		13-year-old son of Harry and Rhoda Brown
Brown, Ira			y		y		7-year-old daughter of Harry and Rhoda Brown
Brown, Jane			y		y		15-year-old daughter of Harry and Rhoda Brown
Brown, Mary			y		y		18-year-old daughter of Harry and Rhoda Brown
Brown, Rhoda			y		y		
Brown, Sarah			y			Slightly	
Brown, W.					y		27 years old; badly wounded
Bullock, Isaac			y				25 years old at time of explosion
Campbell, Duncan		Greenock, Scotland	y	y			A child 2 or 3 years old—parents and family are lost— he was taken to the home of Mr. Henry Smock.
Campbell, Duncan Kelsey		Greenock, Scotland, Bridge of Weir	y		y	Slightly	Infant
Campbell, James		Greenock, Scotland	y	y			25 years old at time of explosion; Mormon
Campbell, Jane		Greenock, Scotland	y	y			Laborer

Name	Title	Origin	LDS	Died*	Wounded	Not Wounded	Notes
Campbell, Neile		Greenock, Scotland	y	y			2 years old
Carter, Isels						y	Br. Woodruff's brother-in-law was on board, on his way to the valley but was not hurt.
Carter, T.J.							
Childers, Thomas		Scotland				y	
Clancey, Josiah	Second Engineer						
Cole, J.							
Conner, John	Watchman				y		He was thrown into the streets of Lexington, yet he lived another 48 years.
Conrad, Peter	Bar-keeper Part Owner					y	
Dilher, G.							
Dunbar, Euphemia		Inverness, Scotland	y	y			6-year-old daughter of William C. and Helen Dunbar
Dunbar, Franklin Lorenzo		Inverness, Scotland	y	y			10-month-old son of William C. and Helen Dunbar
Dunbar, Helen		Inverness, Scotland	y	y			Wife of William C. Dunbar
Dunbar, William		Inverness, Scotland	y		y		Slightly wounded; baptized on 1840; served mission in to England 1846–1852; Emigrated to Utah in 1852; served as mission president of French mission 1854–1855. He was a famous comedian, vocalist, and bagpipe performer of early SLC; founded the Salt Lake Herald; he later died in 1905.
Emory, William	Mate						
Evans, Charles	Carpenter				y		
Evans, John	First Engineer				y	Slightly	
Fale, H.			y			Slightly	
Fireman (black man)							
Fireman (black man)							
Fireman (black man)							
Fireman (white man)					y		
Fireman (white man)					y		
Fireman (white man)					y	y	
Fireman (white man)					y		
Fisher, Abh.							
Foleylimber, Mr.							
Gillespie, Agnes		Scotland	y	y	y		Wife of Alexander Gillespie; her face and neck were badly scalded— taken to Dr. Peebles' house

Name	Title	Origin	LDS	Died*	Wounded	Not Wounded	Notes
Gillespie, Alexander		Scotland	y			y	Later joined the Eli Kelsey wagon train
Gillespie, John		Scotland	y			y	Later joined the Eli Kelsey wagon train
Guerette, Lewis	Second Pilot						
Gunn, H.							
Gunn, Lady							
Hamilton, Mr.							
Harry, Emma		Newport	y	y			Wife of Owen Harry
Harry, Owen O.	Mate	Wales	y		y		Dangerously wounded
Hendley, William						Slightly	
Holmes	Col.	Sullivan, WI				y	
Huff, Thomas						Slightly	
J., Murphy							
Kelsey, Eli			y				Elders in charge of the Saluda migration – took 8 to 10 saints off the boat at Brunswick or Boonville to purchase cattle; later apostatized.
Knapp, Mr.				y			
Kramer, Mr.				y			
Kramer, Mrs.				y			
Kramer, Son				y			
Kramer, Mary					y		Mary Kramer believed she had a brother on the *Saluda*. Lost both of her parents and brother was raised by the Casper Gruber family
La Barge, Charles S.	First Pilot			y			His parents were Joseph Marie La Barge and Evalie Hortiz. He grew up in St. Louis and had 6 siblings, one was Joseph, a famous river captain.
Lamb, Mr.							
Laynell, Mr.	Barkeeper			y			He was the brother of Mrs. Charles La Barge.
Legatt, Mr.				y			
Letcher, Mr.							
Marr, George					y		Left arm amputated
Martin, Abner							
Martin, Lady							
Martin's Servant							
May, Elizabeth			y				Died of Cholera in 1852
May, Emily			y				Died of Cholera in 1852
May, George			y		y		Died of Cholera in 1852

Name	Title	Origin	LDS	Died*	Wounded	Not Wounded	Notes
May, Hannah			y				Died of Cholera in 1852
May, Harriet			y		y		
May, James			y				
May, Richard			y				
May, Thomas			y				Died of Cholera in 1852
May, William			y	y			
McCallister, N.						Slightly	
McGee, W.					y		
McKeachie, Daughter						y	8-year-old daughter; taken to Mr. Geo's home
McKeachie, Daughter						y	3-year-old daughter; taken to Mr. F. Zeiler's home
McKeachie, Sarah					y		spine dangerously injured taken to Prof. Patterson's home
McKeachie, Wilson						y	7 years old: taken to Mr. James Nichols' home
Mitchell, Ann		Chicksaw, Mississippi	y			y	Only child of the Rebecca and John Mitchell that survived
Mitchell, John		Chicksaw, Mississippi	y		y		Left thigh amputated; died shortly afterwards because of the accident.
Mitchell, Josephine		Chicksaw, Mississippi	y	y			Daughter of Rebecca and John T. Mitchell
Mitchell, Preston		Chicksaw, Mississippi	y	y			2-year-old son of Rebecca and John Mitchell
Mitchell, Rebecca Huff		Chicksaw, Mississippi	y			y	Preceded onto Utah Valley with her daughter, Ann Eliza
Mitchell, William		Chicksaw, Mississippi	y	y			4-year-old son of Rebecca and John Mitchell
Murphy, J.		Weston					
Murphy, Lady		Weston					
Murphy, W.							
Murphy's Servant		Weston					
Nash, Mr.				y			
Nash, R.				y			
Payne, J. M.							
Perkinmeyer, Anthony					y		Badly wounded
Pogue, Wesley					y		Broken nose
Randall, Miss							
Rigley, Brother			y				Elder in charge of saints on the Saluda
Roberts, Selina				y			
Roberts, son					y		Badly injured, he died three months later in St. Louis

Name	Title	Origin	LDS	Died*	Wounded	Not Wounded	Notes
Roberts, son				y			
Roberts, son				y			
Roberts, son				y			
Roberts, son				y			
Rose, W.				y			
Ross, David J.			y			Slightly	Elder in charge of the Saluda migration; Apostatized.
Rowland, Ann Eliza			y			y	12-year-old daughter; taken to Mr. A. Huntsberry's home
Rowland, David			y	y			
Rowland, Mary			y		y		5-year-old daughter; taken to Mr. John George's home
Rowland, Rachel			y	y			
Rowland, Rachel Evans			y		y		Leg broken—two children saved, three lost—taken to Mr. A. Huntsberry
Rowland, Sarah			y	y			
Rowland, William, Jr.			y	y			
Rowland, William, Sr.		Welsh	y	y			
Sampson, B.H.							
Sampson, M.							
Sampson, Mr.							
Sane, John B.						y	20 years old; he stayed in Lexington for a year before going to Texas.
Sargent, Ellen			y				She was dopted by a family in Lexington; she married and died by 29.
Sargent, John		Newbury	y	y			Found on the riverbank, dead, stripped, and robbed of his money, John left 3 children.
Sargent, Joseph		Newbury	y				8-year-old son of John Sargent
Sargent, Louisa			y				Continued onto SLC with Sarah and John Jr.
Sargent, Sarah Ann		18 December 1836 England	y			y	Daughter of John Sargent, Sarah met John Martin on her way to a dressmaker's house. He, having been orphaned for twenty years, had been praying to meet a beautiful woman in body and soul. They were married three weeks later.
Shaffer, E.				y			

Name	Title	LDS	Origin	Died*	Wounded	Not Wounded	Notes
Shults							
Shultzer, P.						Slightly	
Shymer, Jas						Slightly	
Sternes, F.					y		
Summerton, John	Saluda Mariner						
Sutton, John P.			Iowa			y	
T.J.			Kanesville				
Tebo, Lewis	Pilot			y			
Tillard, Mr.							
Wag...S.				y			
Wayley					y		
Welch, John					y		
Whitaker, Miss						Slightly	
Whitaker, Sister		y	England	y			
Whitehead, Catherine		y	Birmingham	y			37-year-old wife of George Whitehead
Whitehead, George		y	Birmingham	y			37 years old
Whitehead, George		y	Birmingham	y			16-year-old son of George and Catherine Whitehead
Whitehead, Isabel		y	Birmingham	y			2-year-old daughter of of George and Catherine Whitehead
Whitehead, Mary Gleadhall		y	Birmingham	y			72-year-old Mother of George Whitehead
Wiseman, Matilda						y	Employed to care for the John Sargent children; her fiance was killed in the explosion, but she survived.
Wycuff, Jas			Independence				
Young, Adolphus		y				y	Entire family not injured; later died from cholera while crossing the Nebraska plains
Young, Child		y					Died from cholera while crossing the Nebraska plains
Young, Child		y					Died from cholera while crossing the Nebraska plains
Young, Child		y					Went on to cross the plains
Young, Child		y					Went on to cross the plains
Young, Child		y					Went on to cross the plains
Young, Child		y					Went on to cross the plains
Young, Rhoda		y			y		Went on to cross the plains

*or missing and assumed dead

Bibliography

Newspaper

Church News (Salt Lake City)
Daily Missouri Republican (St. Louis)
Deseret News (Salt Lake City)
Glasgow Weekly Times
Hannibal Weekly Messenger
Jefferson Inquirer Kansas City Journal_Post
Kansas City Star
Kansas City Times
Latter-day Saints' Millennial Star
Lexington Advertiser News
Lexington Weekly Express
Liberty Weekly Tribune
Missouri Reporter (St. Louis)
New York Times

News Tribune (Jefferson City, Missouri)
North Missouri Courier
Ray County Mirror
Richmond Herald
Rural Missouri
Savannah Reporter
Savannah Sentinel
St. Joseph Gazette
St. Joseph New Press
St. Louis Luminary
St. Louis Weekly Reveille
Telegraph
Waterways Journal

Primary Sources

1850 Federal Census for Lafayette County. Elizabeth Ellsbury, comp. Trails Regional Library (Lexington, Missouri).

Baker, Jean Rio Griffiths. Diary. LDS Church Archives.

Ballard, Henry. Reminiscences and Diary. LDS Church Archives.

Guardian's Bond of Alexander McFadden to Duncan Campbell. Lexington Circuit Court.

Harris, George Henry Abbot. Journal. LDS Church Archives.

Higbee, John Sommers. Journal. LDS Church Archives.

Inventory of the State of Duncan Campbell. 22 May 1852. Lexington Circuit Court.

Journal History of the Church. LDS Church Archives.

King, Hannah T. Diary. LDS Church Archives.

Marriage Records Lafayette County 18 October 1866. Lexington, Missouri.

May, James. Journal. LDS Church Archives.

Missouri River Map. Missouri State Historical Society. 8 March 1853.

Probate Records, Lafayette County, Lexington, Missouri.

Saluda Enrollments. Ruth Ferris Collection. Mercantile Library, University of Missouri – St. Louis.

Spiers, John. Journal. LDS Church Archives.

St. Louis Steamboat Enrollment, no. 99. Ruth Ferris Collection. Mercantile Library, University of Missouri - St. Louis.

Steamboat Tickets, replicas. Battle of Lexington State Historic Site.

Steamer Fare "Elvira." Western Historical Manuscript Collection. St. Genevieve Archive Collection 3636, fd 1212.

Steamer Fare "Julia Chouteau." Western Historical Manuscript Collection. St. Genevieve Archive Collection 3636, fd 1004.

Tyler, Daniel. Journal. LDS Church Archives.

United States Congress, *The Congressional Globe*, (Washington: Blair & Rives: 1834-1873).

Young, Brigham. Incoming and outgoing correspondence in the Brigham Young Papers. LDS Church Archives.

Books

1997-1998 Church Almanac. Salt Lake City, UT: Deseret News Publishing Company, 1996.

Arrington, Leonard, ed. *The Presidents of the Church : Biographical Essays.* Salt Lake City, UT: Deseret Book, 1986.

Brightly, Frederick C. *An Analytical Digest of the Laws of the United States.* Philadelphia: Kay & Brother, 1857-1869.

Brunner, John. *The Great Steamboat Race.* New York: Ballantine Books, 1983.

Chappell, Phil E. *A History of the Missouri River: Discovery of the River by the Jesuit Explorers; Indian Tribes Along the River; Early Navigation and Craft Used; The Rise and Fall of Steamboating.* Kansas City, MO: Bryant & Douglas Book and Stationery Co., 1911.

Chittenden, Hiram Martin. *History of Early Steamboat Navigation on the Missouri River.* Minneapolis: Ross & Haines, 1962.

Coleman, Terry. *Passage to America: A History of Emigrants from Great Britain and Ireland to America in the Mid-nineteenth Century.* London: Hutchinson of London, 1972.

Conclin, George. *Conclins' New River Guide, or A Gazetteer of All the Towns on the Western Waters.* Cincinnati: J.A. & U.P. James, 1853.

Connelley, William Elsey. *A Standard History of Kansas and Kansans.* 5 vols. Chicago and New York: Lewis Publishing Company, 1918.

Death Records of Missouri Men: From Newspapers 1808-1854. George F. Wilson, Maryhelen Wilson, and Lois Stanley, comp. 1981.

Dennis, Ronald D. *The Call of Zion: The Story of the First Welsh Mormon Emigration.* 2 vols. Provo, UT: Religious Studies Center Brigham Young University, 1987.

Diary of a Town Wellington, Missouri. Joanne Chiles Eakin, comp. Independence, MO: Wee Print, 1984.

Drago, Harry Sinclair. *The Steamboaters: From the Early Side-wheelers to the Big Packets.* New York: Dodd, Mead, and Company, 1967.

Early Members of the Reorganized Church of Jesus Christ of Latter-day Saints. Susan Easton Black, comp. 6 vols. Provo, UT: Religious Studies Center Brigham Young University, 1993.

Ekin, Charles, ed. *Diary of a Town, Wellington, Missouri.* Garr, Arnold K., Donald Q. Cannon, Richard O. Cowan, Richard Neitzel Holzapfel, eds. *Latter-day Saint Church History Encyclopedia.* Salt Lake City, UT: Deseret Book Company, 2000.

Gillespie, Michael. *Wild River, Wooden Boats: True Stories of Steamboating and the Missouri River.* Stoddard, WI: Heritage Press, 2000.

Gould, E. W. *Fifty Years On the Mississippi or Gould's History of River Navigation.* St. Louis, MO: Nixon-Jones Printing Company, 1889.

Hawthorne, Nathaniel. *The English Notebooks.* Ed. Randall Stewart. New York: Oxford University Press, 1941.

Heninger, Hattie Elizabeth Walton. *A Brief Historical and Genealogical Account of the Walton Family in the New England States, the Western States, and Canada, With Notes on Some of the Allied Families.* Salt Lake City, UT: Hattie E. Walton Heninger, 1971.

History of Lafayette County, Missouri. St. Louis: Missouri Historical Company, 1882.

Hunter, Louis C. *Steamboats on the Western Rivers: An Economical and Technological History.* New York: Octagon Books, 1969.

Jenson, Andrew. *Church Chronology: A Record of Important Events.* Salt Lake City, UT: Deseret News, 1899.

Jenson, Andrew. *Encyclopedia History of the Church of Jesus Christ of Latter-day Saints.* Salt Lake City, UT: Deseret News Publishing Company, 1941. Jenson, Andrew. *Latter-day Saint Biographical Encyclopedia.* Salt Lake City, UT: Andrew Jenson History Company, 1901.

Kimball, Stanley B. *Historic Resource Study: Mormon Pioneer National Historic Trail.* United States Department of Interior/National Park Service, 1991.

The Holy Bible : authorized King James version with explanatory notes and cross references to the standard works of the Church of Jesus Christ of Latter-day Saints. Salt Lake City, Utah : Church of Jesus Christ of Latter-Day Saints, 1987.

Larson, Ron. *Upper Mississippi River History: Fact-Fiction-Legend.* Winona, MN: Steamboat Press, 1994.

Linforth, James, ed. *Route From Liverpool to Great Salt Lake Valley With Steel Engravings and Woodcuts from Sketches made by Frederick Piercy.* Liverpool: Franklin D. Richards, 1855. Little, B.M. *The National Old Trails Road and Part Played by Lexington in the Westward Movement.* B. M. Little, 1928.

Lloyd, James T. *Lloyd's Steamboat Directory: Disaster on the Western Waters.* Cincinnati: James T. Lloyd and Company, 1856.

McCutcheon, Marc. *The Writer's Guide to Everyday Life in the 1800s.* Cincinnati: Writer's Digest Books, 1993.

McDermott, John Francis, ed. *Before Mark Twain: A Sampler of Old, Old Times on the Mississippi.* Carbondale and Edwardsville: Southern Illinois University Press, 1968.

Melville, Herman. *Redburn: His First Voyage.* Boston: St. Boltolph Society, 1924.

Membership of the Church of Jesus Christ of Latter-day Saints. Susan Easton Black, comp. 50 vols. Provo, UT: Religious Studies Center Brigham Young University, 1989.

O'Neil, Paul. *The Old West: The Rivermen.* New York: Time-Life Books, 1975.

Our Pioneer Heritage. Kate B. Carter, comp. 20 vols. Salt Lake City, UT: Daughters of Utah Pioneers, 1958-1977.

Primm, James Neal. *Lion of the Valley: St. Louis, Missouri, 1764-1980.* 3d ed. St. Louis, MO: Missouri Historical Society Press, 1998.

Reader's Digest, Story of the Great American West. Pleasantville, New York: Reader's Digest Assn., 1977.

Riddle, Chauncey Cazier, and Bertha Allred Riddle, eds. *Isaac Riddle and His Family.* Provo, UT: Riddle Family, 1990.

Roberts, B.H. *A Comprehensive History of The Church of Jesus Christ of Latter-day Saints.* 6 vols. Provo, UT: Brigham Young University Press, 1965.

Sellers, Katherine Wilson. *Historical Glimpses of Lexington.* Lexington Library and Historical Association, 1980.

Shoemaker, Floyd. *Missouri, Day by Day.* Jefferson City, MO: State Historical Society of Missouri: Mid-State Printing Co., 1942-43.

Smoot, Loretta D. and L. Douglas Smoot. *Abraham Owen Smoot: A Testament of His Life.* Provo, UT: Brigham Young Press, 1994.

Sonne, Conway B. *Saints on the Seas: A Maritime History of Mormon Migration, 1830-1890.* Salt Lake City, UT: University of Utah Press, 1983.

Sonne, Conway B. *Ships, Saints, and Mariners: a Maritime Encyclopedia of Mormon Migration, 1830-1890.* Salt Lake City, UT: University of Utah Press, 1987.

Stevens, Walter B. *St. Louis, The Fourth City, 1764-1909.* St. Louis: S. J. Clarke Publishing Co., 1909. Swift, James V. *Backing Hard Into River History.* Florissant, MO: A Little River Book, 2001.

The Doctrine and Covenants of The Church of Jesus Christ of Latter-day Saints. Salt Lake City, UT: The Church of Jesus Christ of Latter-day Saints, 1981.

Tombstone Inscriptions of Lafayette County, Missouri. Marty Helm Brunetti, comp. 3 vols. Warrensburg, MO: Marty Helm Brunetti, 1977.

Trager, James. *The People's Chronology: A Year-by-Year Record of Human Events from Prehistory to the Present.* Rev. and up. ed. New York: Henry Holt and Company, 1992.

Twain, Mark. *Life on the Mississippi.* New York: Airmont Publishing Company, 1965.

Unruh, John, Jr. *The Plains Across: The Overland Immigrants and the Trans-Mississippi West, 1840-1860.* Urbana and Chicago: University of Illinois Press, 1979.

Way, Frederick, Jr. *Way's Packet Directory, 1848-1994: Passenger Steamboats of the Mississippi River System Since the Advent of Photography in Mid-continent America.* rev. ed. Athens, OH: Ohio University, 1983.

Wayman, Norbury L. *Life on the River: A Pictorial History of the Mississippi, The Missouri, and the Western River System.* New York: Crown Publishers, Inc., 1971.

Williams, Neville. *Chronology of World History Volume III 1776-1900, The Changing World.* 3 vols. Santa Barbara: ABC-CLIO, Inc., 1999.

Williams, Walter, ed. *A History of Northwest Missouri.* 3 vols. Chicago and New York: Lewis Publishing Company, 1915.

Woodruff, Wilford. *Annual Conference of the 1898 Annual Conference of the Church of Jesus Christ of Latter-day Saints.* Salt Lake City, UT: The Church of Jesus Christ of Latter-day Saints, 1898.

Woodruff, Wilford. *Wilford Woodruff's Journal, 1833-1898.* Ed. Scott G. Kenney. 9 vols. Midvale, UT: Signature Books, 1983-1984.

Young, Rhoda Byrne Jared. *The Book of Jared.* Comp. Eleanor McAllister Hall. 1963.

Young, William. *Lafayette County Missouri.* 2 vols. Indianapolis: B. F. Bowen & Company, 1910.

Young, William. *Young's History of Lafayette County Missouri.* Indianapolis: B.F. Bowen and Company, 1910.

Articles

"Editor's Table." *Harper's New Monthly Magazine* (June - November 1852): 83-842.

"News of the Church: Saluda Victims Remembered." *Ensign* (January 1992): 78.

Allen, James B. and Malcolm R. Thorp. "The Mission of the Twelve to England, 1840-41: Mormon Apostles and the Working Classes." *BYU Studies* 15 (summer 1975): 499-526.

Barry, Louise, ed., "Overland to the Gold fields of California in 1852: the journal of John Hawkins Clark," *The Kansas State Historical Quarterly* 11 (August 1942):228-296.

Berbert, Geri. "Disaster on the Mississippi." *Ensign* (September 1981): 26-30.

Blair, Roger P. "The Doctor Gets Some Practice: Cholera and Medicine on the Overland Trails." *Journal of the West* 34 (January 1997): 54-66.

Buchanan, Frederick S. "The Ebb and Flow of the Church in Scotland, 1840-1900." *BYU Studies* 27 (Spring 1987): 27-52.

Buice, David. "When the Saints Came Marching In: The Mormon Experience in Antebellum New Orleans, 1840-1855." *Louisiana History* 23 (summer 1982): 221-237.

Curtis, Annette. "Explosion of the Steamship Saluda." *The Kansas City Genealogist* 34 (1994).

Dunlop, Richard. "Bound for the Wild Missouri." *Reader's Digest* (September 1985): 149-155.

Espenschied, Lloyd. "Louis Espenschied and His Family." *The Bulletin: Missouri Historical Society* 18 (January 1962): 86-103.

Ferris, Ruth. "Grave Revelations." *Missouri Historical Society Bulletin* 20 (April 1964).

Gerber, Rudolph J. "Old Woman River." *Missouri Historical Review* 56 (July 1962).

Gray, Jacki. "Tragedy Aboard the *Saluda.*" *Rural Missouri* 38 (August 1985).

Hartley, William G. "St. Louis and the Nauvoo Exodus: The Experiences of the John Ellison Family." *Nauvoo Journal* 19 (Fall 1998): 39-48.

Hawley, Gregory L. and William G. Hartley. "Before the *Arabia* Sank: Mormon Passengers up the Missouri in 1856." *Nauvoo Journal* 10 (Fall 1998): 109-130.

Jenson, Andrew. "Fifty-Sixth Company—*Kennebec.*" *The Contributor* 13 (July 1892): 408-414.

Kimball, Stanley B. "The Saints and St. Louis, 1831-1857: An Oasis of Tolerance and Security." *BYU Studies* 13 (Summer 1973): 489-519.

MacDonald, W. J. "The Missouri River and Its Victims." *The Missouri Historical Review* 21 (July 1927): 581-593.

McLeod, Dean L. "James Ross: The Experiences of a Scottish Immigrant to America." *Family Heritage* 1 (December 1978): 178-179, 182-183.

Priddy, Bob. A Tale of Rashness and Avarice." *Missouri Life* (July - August 1982).

Ravensway, Charles Van. "Years of Turmoil, Years of Growth: St. Louis in the 1850's." *The Bulletin: Missouri Historical Society* 23 (July 1967).

Saddler, Richard W. "Franklin D. Richards and the British Mission." *Journal of Mormon History* 14 (1988): 81-95.

Taylor, Phillip A. M. "Mormons and Gentiles on the Atlantic." *Utah Historical Society* 24 (July 1956): 195-204.

Woods, Fred E. "East to West through North and South: Mormon Immigration during the Civil War." *BYU Studies* 39 (winter 2000): 7-29.

Woods, Fred E. "More Precious Than Gold: The Rush To and Through Zion 1849-50." *Nauvoo Journal* 11 (spring 1999): 109-124.

Woods, Fred E. "Two Sides of a River: Mormon Transmigration through Quincy, Illinois, and Hannibal, Missouri." *Mormon Historical Studies* 2 (spring 2001): 119-147.

Wyman, Walker Demarquis. "Council Bluffs and the Westward Movement." *Iowa Journal of History* 47 (April 1949): 99-118.

Unpublished Works

Bashore, Melvin L. Email to William Hartley and Fred Woods. 21 February 2002. Copy in the authors' files.

Callister, Beth Hutchings. "The Story of Matilda Wiseman Hutchings." Unpublished memoirs in possession of Fred E. Woods, courtesy of Gene Hutchings.

Coleman, Thomas. Letter to Dear Father. 14 April 1852. In Coleman-Hayter, Letters, 1840-1900. Special Collections Library, University of Missouri–St. Louis.

Day, Robert O. and Linda Day. "The Steamboat Saluda Disaster." 8 pp. typescript, April 1992. Copy in White's *Saluda* files, Ogden, Utah.

Ferrin, Lettie Saunders Taylor. *Impressions about the Harris Family.* Unpublished memoirs about Martin Henderson Harris and Louisa Sargent Harris, 23 May 1953.

Hartley, William G. "'Don't Go Aboard the *Saluda.*'" 11 pp. typescript, June 1983.

Hokanson, Paul. E-mail to Fred Woods. 21 February 2002. Copy in the author's file.

Jenson, Andrew. *Church Emigration Book, 1850-54.* Salt Lake City, UT: Church Historical Department, Library Division, 1852.

Platte, O. V. Cecil. "The Saluda." a poem.

Schaperkotter, Pete. Letter to Ruth M. White. 22 September 1990. In White's *Saluda* files, Ogden, Utah.

Slusher, Roger. *Lexington: A Brief History.* 3 pp. typescript. Copy in authors' possession.

Sonne, Conway B. "Liverpool and the Mormon Emigration." Paper presented at the Mormon History Association Conference in Liverpool, England, 10 July 1987.

Spies, Dan. "The Story of the *Saluda.*" Unpublished paper from the University of Missouri Arts and Science papers, 1908-1965, in Columbia, Missouri.

White, Ruth M. Letter to Norma N. King. 5 December 1998. Copy in White's *Saluda* files, Ogden, Utah.

White, Ruth McFarland and Lois Belnap Erickson. "John Sargent and his family or the Tale of Two Sisters." Unpublished document in possession of Jeane Burton.

Index

Gaunt, George W. 33

Gillespie, Agnes 39, 45

Gillespie, Alexander 24, 39

Gillespie, John 24, 39, 40

Gold Rush 1, 20, 24, 57

Gratz, H. H. 46

Great Britain 62, 81

Griffiths, Jean Rio 8, 9, 11, 20

Guerette, Louis 14, 35, 55

Hale, Colonel James 31, 35

Harris, George Henry Abbot 80

Harry, Owen 38, 45

Harry, Emma 38

Hawthorne, Nathaniel 82

Hemler, William 14, 15, 32, 45, 55

Higbee, John S. 4, 10, 12, 13,
    14, 48

Hudgens, Prince L. 61

Isabel 25-26, 31-34, 37, 40, 42, 48,
    66-67, 69-70, 72

Jenson, Andrew 82, 85

Kanesville, Iowa 18

Kelsey, Eli B. 2, 3, 12, 13, 24,
    39, 40, 48, 49, 50, 53, 58, 63, 64

Kennebec 1-2, 4, 9-13, 49, 66, 69,
    85

Kirtland Ohio 7

La Barge, Charles 14, 33, 55

La Barge, Joseph 14, 20

Linforth, James 82

Liverpool 1, 4, 7, 9, 59, 82, 86

May, George 24, 31, 32, 37,
    45, 48, 58

May, James 10, 24, 31, 32, 37, 45,
    48, 58, 80

McKeachie, Sarah 45

McKenzie, Thomas 11

Millennial Star 9, 11, 59, 80

Miller, Captain William B.
    25, 31, 32, 40, 42

Mississippi River, 5, 11-12, 15, 18,
    23, 60, 82-83

Missouri River, 0-2, 6-7, 15, 17-20,
    22-24, 34, 42, 49, 55-58, 61, 65,
    68-69, 80-82, 85

Mitchell, Ann Eliza 31

Mitchell, John Tillery 31, 38, 45

Mitchell, Josephine 31

Mitchell, Preston 31

Mitchell, Rebecca 31

Mitchell, William 31

Nauvoo, Illinois 7-8

New Orleans 1, 4, 6-7, 10-13, 20,
    31, 59, 84

Planter 42